The New York Times

ON THE
SOPRANOS

AVAILABLE NOW

AMOS WALKER MYSTERIES
Motor City Blue
by Loren D. Estleman

SHERLOCK HOLMES MYSTERIES
Revenge of the Hound
by Michael Hardwick

PHILIP MARLOWE MYSTERIES
Raymond Chandler's Philip Marlowe
Anthology; Byron Preiss, Editor

COMING SOON

Angel Eyes
An Amos Walker Mystery
by Loren D. Estleman

MOSES WINE MYSTERIES
The Big Fix
by Roger L. Simon

The Lost Coast
by Roger L. Simon

TOBY PETERS MYSTERIES
Murder on the Yellow Brick Road
by Stuart Kaminsky

The Devil Met a Lady
by Stuart Kaminsky

Share your thoughts about these and other ibooks titles
in the new ibooks virtual reading group at
www.ibooksinc.com

The New York Times
ON THE SOPRANOS

INTRODUCTION BY
STEPHEN HOLDEN

AFTERWORD BY
STEPHEN J. CANNELL

This book has not been prepared, approved, or licensed by any entity that created or produces The Sopranos and is unaffiliated with HBO and Chase Films.

ibooks
new york
www.ibooksinc.com

Contents

THE SOPRANOS:

AN INTRODUCTION

by Stephen Holden

Early last year, as word began to spread that the Home Box Office series *The Sopranos* was not only the best television drama ever made, but episode by episode as good or better than any Hollywood movie to be released in ages, people who had never considered ordering a cable channel scrambled to subscribe to Home Box Office to see what the fuss was about.

What they discovered, along with the millions who were already hooked on the series, was richly textured comic realism of a complexity and truthfulness that had never before been seen on television, not even in such beloved British series as *Upstairs Downstairs, Brideshead Revisited and I, Claudius.*

The brainchild of the writer-director David Chase, *The Sopranos* in its 13 first-season episodes follows the fortunes of the Sopranos, an upper-middle class New Jersey clan whose paterfamilias Tony Soprano just happens to be a local Mafia kingpin. The series deals head on with questions about family, community, crime, and ethics that not even *The Godfather* films, which brought new level of tragic realism to cinema in the 1970's dared address.

The short answer to those questions, which are concerned with the integration of criminal life and a so-called "normal" life is that it's not that big a deal. For *The Sopranos* subscribes unblinkingly to the absurd view of history, which is the version that most of us live by even if we don't know it. In the absurd view of life, it's people's little quirks and kinks that make big things to happen. Modern wars and coups are just as likely to be the products of mood swings, temper tantrums, ruffled pride and childish score-settling as the outcomes of ideological and spiritual crusades. After all, hasn't the world always had its share of Caligula-like despots who rule without rhyme or reason and sometimes destroy whole societies?

The Caligula-like despot in *The Sopranos* is Tony's widowed mother Livia, an ominous matriarch who subtly coerces her mobster brother-in-law Junior to take out a contract on Tony's life. Why would a mother do such a thing? Out of paranoia and spite, it turns out. She resents him for pressuring her to leave the home she is no longer able to manage and go live in ritzy retirement home which he pays for but which she believes to be a nursing home. On learning that Tony has been seeing a psychiatrist, Livia is seized with the outraged certainty that he spends his therapy sessions denouncing her.

Tony's uncle Junior, who orders the hit, is as believably crazy in his way as Livia is in hers. When his loyal longtime girlfriend boasts in a nail salon of Junior's prowess at performing oral sex, the news filters back to Tony who mercilessly ribs Junior about bedroom etiquette that Tony and his macho cronies scorn as unmanly. Junior's humiliation and fury seriously deepens the potentially murderous breach between uncle and nephew.

Over the course of 13 hour-long episodes, these and other wounds accumulate the force of Greek tragedy. Or is it a Chekhov comedy replayed in the foul-mouthed street language of New Jersey hoodlums? For if the The Sopranos is often laugh-out-loud funny, the laughter it elicits doesn't come from one-liners but from a deeper recognition of the screaming little baby inside every grownup.

The Sopranos, more than any American television show, looks, feels and sounds like real life as it's lived experienced in the United States in the cluttered environment of the Internet, mall shopping, rap music and a runaway stock market. Watch any episode and you're likely to come away with the queasy feeling of consuming a greasy slice of here and now with its surreal mixture of prosperity and brutishness. Tony's New Jersey mob boss isn't an exotic evil king holed up in a fortified stone castle. He is a harried forty-something middle-class Joe who, except for his occupation, is not all that different from the rest of us.

The Sopranos, sustains its hyper-realism with an eye and ear so exquisitely attuned to contemporary culture and social niceties that it just might be the greatest work of American popular culture of the last quarter century. It was in 1974 that the second of The Godfather movies was released. Together with its 1971 forerunner, it gave American culture a new myth, inspired by the 20th-century immigrant experience to replace the old one of the frontier and the winning of the west. *The Sopranos* carries *The Godfather* movies' epic vision into the present, turning tragedy into comedy and vice versa.

The series' greatness lies in its creation of at least a dozen indelible characters whom we come to know as intimately as close friends. At the center looms James Gandolfini's Tony, a hairy-shouldered grizzly bear who loves his wife Carmela and teenage children (the obedient Meadow and the rowdy Tony, Jr.), who watches the History Channel and blows off steam by pumping iron in the basement of his New Jersey home. Out of the blue one day, Tony starts suffering devastating panic attacks. When it's discovered there's nothing physically wrong with him, he begins to see Dr. Jennifer Melfi (Lorraine Bracco), a local psychiatrist recommended by the doctor who lives next door.

There are two essentially two Tonys. One is a mobster involved in theft, loan-sharking, drugs, and corrupt unions. This Tony takes brutal relish in beating up and killing those who cross him. The other Tony is a strait-laced family man who frets that his two children have discovered he isn't really in "waste management" as he claims. This is the same Tony who flares up when his daughter brings up sex at the dinner table and announces that in his house it is still 1954. Yet this devoted family man is also part owner of a topless bar and has a girl-friend who is a Russian prostitute.

The criminal Tony and the righteous Tony become grotesquely connected after a soccer coach in his daughter's high school impregnates one of her friends. The moralistic Tony goes ballistic. The criminal Tony considers enlisting his cronies to carry out a savage act of vigilante justice.

Along with Gandolfini and Marchand, Edie Falco (as the loyal but sharp-tongued Carmela). Bracco, and Michael Imperioli who plays Christopher Moltisanti, Tony's dumb, hot-headed nephew, who itches to be a "made" member of the Mafia, have the roles of their lifetimes in the series.

In many ways, *The Sopranos*, more the wobbly, histrionic *Godfather, Part 3*, is the real sequel to Francis Ford Coppola's *Godfather* movies, which evoked the rise of Mafia in America as a parallel shadow image of corporate America. *The Sopranos* flagrantly borrows such dramatic techniques from *The Godfather* movies as crosscutting between scenes of extreme violence and domestic warmth, and interspersing the narrative with semi-hallucinatory flashbacks.

The thugs, especially Christopher, are so entranced with the mystique of *The Godfather* that they quote (and sometimes misquote) its dialogue. Christopher impatiently aspires to the imperial glamor of Marlon Brando and Al Pacino, and one episode finds him working on an inept screenplay about mob life in the absurd assumption that a screenwriting and acting career are just around the corner.

But as much it owes to *The Godfather*, *The Sopranos* also refutes the towering solemnity of the Francis Ford Coppola films. Tony and his pals have none of the royal demeanor of *The Godfather's* kingpins. Most are crude, bigoted, semi-literate boors who seem slightly out of place in the contemporary world. The criminal world in

The Sopranos is strictly small potatoes, and it's fading. Tony, who's smarter than his colleagues, realizes that this seamy little society with its grim Old World code of loyalty, is becoming obsolescent, but there's not much he can do about it. *The Godfather's* Corleones were made of sterner stuff. Even in their worst nightmares, they wouldn't dream of taking their problems to a shrink.

Some of *The Sopranos*' finest scenes take place in Dr. Melfi's office. Bracco's cool-headed psychiatrist drops all the right buzzwords, gently prodding her client toward insights into his childhood and his relationship with his parents, and dispensing anti-depressants and tranquilizers when needed. Her give-and-take with Tony may be the most realistic depiction of therapy ever depicted in a mainstream movie or television show.

Tony even develops a classic case of transference (drawn out in eerie, erotic dream sequences) in which he briefly imagines he's in love with the doctor. But *The Sopranos* ultimately dismystifies psychotherapy as much as it does the world of *The Godfather*. Psychotherapy proves useful for Tony (it supplies him with some clever managerial strategies), but it hasn't the slightest impact on his criminal character.

In forcing us to empathize with a thug whom we watch committing heinous acts, *The Sopranos* evokes a profound moral ambiguity. One of the series' most haunting moments finds Tony's teenage daughter Meadow crouched on the stairs furtively watching her parents remove guns and cash from a hiding place in preparation for an imminent search by federal agents. How does a nice middle-class teenager deal with the fact that her adored father is a thief and a killer? In the first season's most poignant moment, she bluntly inquires, "Dad, are you in the Mafia?" during a car trip to Maine where she and Tony are visiting colleges (and he slips off at one point to murder an FBI informant he happens to see at a gas station).

The Sopranos walks a fine line. As much as it banalizes its mobsters, it refuses to trivialize their viciousness. Tony's brutality is all the more disturbing because its erupts from within a social framework of apparent normalcy. That framework includes a devout young priest, who like Dr. Melfi, skillfully sidesteps the deeper moral issues of Tony's life. The closest Tony comes to admitting evil is during a therapy session in which he offers the lame excuse that what he does is no worse than a businessman illegally dumping toxic waste.

But isn't that how we all get by in without tearing ourselves to pieces? For aren't all values relative? In a such a moral climate where everything is viewed on a sliding scale, it's easy for Tony to excuse himself, and say, adopting his best macho swagger, "You gotta do what you gotta do."

The New York Times

ON THE
SOPRANOS

EVEN A MOBSTER NEEDS SOMEONE TO TALK TO

by Charles Strum

The concept for the new hour-long HBO series "The Sopranos" sounds simple enough: an upwardly mobile Mafia capo from North Jersey slams head-on into a midlife crisis, enters therapy and starts taking Prozac.

Funny? Sometimes. Scary? Sure. Human? Very. But simple? No. It's about as simple as trying to dispose of a fresh corpse in the Meadowlands after dark when the lip of the construction Dumpster is just too high to reach.

"I was looking for the notion that life is so complex now that even a wiseguy needs help sorting it out," says David Chase, the creator, writer and co-executive producer of the series. "Plus, the mob as we know it has taken some pretty heavy hits from law enforcement. On a realistic level, who's to say that a man involved in this wouldn't be feeling tremendous pressure?"

That man is Tony Soprano (James Gandolfini), and for 13 weeks, starting with the show's premiere [in the first season], the stress of heading two families, the one he lives with and the one he works with, is bared to his psychiatrist and the eavesdropping television audience. The audience sees Tony in all his many guises, including the inner Tony, a man not fully understood by his wife, his girlfriend, his passive-aggressive mother or his two teen-age children.

But help comes from one of his own, an Italian-American therapist. She is Dr. Jennifer Melfi, a new kind of role for Lorraine Bracco, one of the movie screen's more famous mob wives. (Ms. Bracco portrayed Karen Hill, wife of the mobster Henry Hill in "Goodfellas.") Having lived through Mafia home life, Ms. Bracco suddenly finds herself in designer suits and eyeglasses, asking questions like, "How does that make you feel?"

In preparation, she said, she thumbed through books with titles like "Going Sane," "Sexual Feelings in Psychotherapy," "The Intimate Hour" and "The Drama of the Gifted Child."

Tony is a gifted child?

"Of course he's gifted," Ms. Bracco fairly shouted.

"It's heartbreaking," she said. "How could you not like a man who is searching to do the right thing? It's 'Father Knows Best' for the millennium. Tony comes to me with these mother issues, a powerful grown man crying about not knowing what to do."

His wife and his daughter are at each other's throats and his mother, Livia (Nancy Marchand in a startling departure from her famous WASP roles), dispenses guilt with the skill that comes only from generations of genetic honing.

How can any therapist possibly break through? Tony is a guy. A big Italian guy. He has big cars and a big white modern suburban house with a circular drive and a big in-ground pool, plenty of money (cash, usually) and more on the way.

Then comes the panic attack, and he ends up on the couch.

"Lately I get the feeling that I came in at the end," he tells Dr. Melfi, speaking of his work, his life, the really important challenges that confronted his father's generation. "The best is over."

"Are you depressed?" Dr. Melfi asks. Tony demurs, then fumes.

"Whatever happened to Gary Cooper, the strong silent type?" he says. "That was an American. He wasn't in touch with his feelings. He just did what he had to do. See, what they didn't know is that once they got Gary Cooper in touch with his feelings they couldn't get him to shut up. It's dysfunction this, dysfunction that."

As for Tony's ostensible career as a "waste management consultant," Dr. Melfi is cautious. As her patient starts to explain the stress of a recent business transaction—"We saw this guy, and there was this issue of an outstanding loan"—Dr. Melfi interrupts to point out that anything discussed in her office is private, but that if he were to reveal something about, say, a murder, she would be obliged to go to the authorities.

"I don't know what happened with this fellow," Dr. Melfi starts to say, but then Tony breaks in with a sincere smile.

"Nothing," he says, pausing. "We had coffee." At which point the camera leaves Tony's face and refocuses on an office park in Paramus, N.J., where the delinquent debtor, having spotted Tony, drops his tray of takeout coffee and tries unsuccessfully to escape Tony's fists and feet. All in a day's work, which frequently provides evidence of Tony's tough—even inventive—side. At one point, the assaults another wiseguy, using a staple gun to fasten the man's jacket to his chest.

For Dr. Melfi, the brutal Tony is not such a big issue.

"Look, I can only approach it in a way that is best for him clinically, medically," Ms. Bracco said. "Getting into a discussion of stapling the guy's suit to him is not going to help me crack his psyche open to see the good and evil."

Ms. Bracco originally read not for this quiet, contemplative part, but for Carmela, Tony's wife, played by Edie Falco.

"Actors, we want roles that chew the scenery up," Ms. Bracco said. "But I was interested in a character no one has given me before. She's so controlled. She's a blank wall. This is almost like not speaking.

"She's not just a psychiatrist, she's from the neighborhood, you know? How many many Italian-American educated women have you seen on screen?"

Ms. Bracco grew up in Bay Ridge, Brooklyn; her "big, powerful Italian father" worked at the Fulton Fish Market. As Dr. Melfi, she reins in the street-corner Brooklyn dialect that is her customary way of chatting.

Which leads to the question of Italians and stereotyping, and whether "The Sopranos" is likely to come in for some criticism.

Mr. Chase, whose family name was originally DeCesare, and the HBO-Brillstein Grey Entertainment production team see no problem. Neither do the cast members, almost all of whom are Italian-Americans from the New York-New Jersey area. Mr. Chase grew up in

North Caldwell, N.J., in Essex County, where the Sopranos live, and insisted on filming at locations throughout northern New Jersey.

Mr. Gandolfini called the show an "equal opportunity drama."

"Certain things lend themselves to drama," he said. "It didn't bother me at all. I think people are ready for a certain lack of political correctness. We do things with some respect."

It also appears to be true to mob life in the 90's and the notion that art imitates life imitating art; that is, today's gangsters like to model themselves after their screen idols. The series is peppered with overused epigrams from Hollywood mob melodramas. In the scene in which Christopher (Michael Imperioli) and his partner (Vincent Pastore) try to dispose of a body in the Meadowlands, Christopher intones, "Louis Brasi sleeps with the fishes."

"Luca Brasi, Luca, Christopher," the partner corrects.

Celebrating a big cash haul at Newark International Airport, another crew member, Paulie (Tony Sirico), invokes Edward G. Robinson when he exults dramatically but pointlessly, "Is this the end of Little Rico?"

And crew members analyzing a recent rubout ruminate on the significance of killing someone by shooting him in the eye. Citing primary source material, they discuss the death of the casino owner Moe Green in "The Godfather."

"It's so funny because it's so real," said Chris Albrecht, president of HBO Original Programming. "These characters are all completely relatable. The only difference between Tony Soprano and me is that he's a mob boss."

Is Tony Soprano not so different from the Wall Street sharks who live down the block? Perhaps only in that he carries a .45 and they don't.

"I understand him," said Mr. Gandolfini, who grew up in Park Ridge, in North Jersey. "He can be brutal and compassionate. I think that people who have a lot of compassion also have a lot of anger. With some people the anger gets stuck."

Yet the compassionate side is often within reach.

In midseries, Tony and his 17-year-old daughter, Meadow, drive to Maine to visit colleges. Cruising along in the family's light-gray Lincoln, a pensive Meadow suddenly turns to her father and asks, "Are you in the Mafia?"

"Am I in the what?" Tony says. "That's total crap—who told you that? That's a stereotype, and it's offensive. I'm in the waste management business. Everybody immediately assumes you're mobbed up. There is no Mafia."

But Tony's practiced lying is momentary, and he relents with one of the few people in the world he loves unconditionally.

"Look," he says, "some of my money comes from illegal gambling and whatnot." A pause. "How does that make you feel?"

"Sometimes," Meadow says wistfully, "I wish you were like other dads." But she has already inherited the Soprano coyness. She just needed to hear it from him.

Later, at dinner, the conversation continues, and in a single moment, with his daughter's face shining in the candlelight of a restaurant, Tony the son, Tony the father and Tony the striver merge to confront the newly self-absorbed Tony.

"My father was in it, my uncle was in it," he says. "There was a time there when the Italian people didn't have a lot of options."

"Maybe," he adds, "being a rebel in my family would have been selling patio furniture on Route 22."

—January 3, 1999

LOCATION, LOCATION; 'THE SOPRANOS' TUNES IN TO A NEW JERSEY NOBODY KNOWS (EXCEPT FOR THE MILLIONS WHO CALL IT HOME)

by Charles Strum

Something unforeseen happened in January [1999] when a new television series became a hit: New Jersey became a star.

Not just the idea of New Jersey, or an extended riff on the jokes about New Jersey: its web of highways, nests of foundries or pools of toxic water beside the tank farms and generating plants. The New Jersey where people live, work and prosper finally got a fair shake.

The show is "The Sopranos" on HBO. Granted, it's about a mob boss jousting with the demons of middle age, a dark comedy with overtones of brutality. But it's also very much about a place—with moods and textures, hard and soft, inviting and repellent, silly and sophisticated. It's not about public relations. The vast green marshes of the Meadowlands also contain Dumpsters and corpses. Truck depots and abandoned waterfronts look as gritty as they are. A shimmering notion of Manhattan—a better, grander place?—is just over the horizon (Route 3 to the Lincoln, Route 4 to the G.W.B.)

But perhaps for the first time in a weekly series, New Jersey is more than just the way to someplace else, an overhead turnpike sign or a dismissive line in the script.

Suddenly, towns like Kearny, Harrison and Belleville, rural backwaters before the Industrial Revolution, are seen as the working-class mini-metropolises they are, cramped but still vital communities of two-and-three-story houses and stores hemmed in by train tracks and old rivers.

Paramus, West Orange, Wayne, North Caldwell, Bloomfield, almost two dozen communities so far, have permitted their homes, office parks, storefronts, warehouses and restaurants to serve not just as backdrops but as themselves. You may not always know which town you're looking at, but that lawn is somebody's lawn, that house is somebody's house and, more often than not, that school or hospital or warehouse is bona fide New Jersey.

The force behind the authenticity is David Chase, the creator, writer and occasionally director of the series. He lives in Los Angeles now, but he's a Jersey guy, and he tells a cautionary tale about the first network to consider the show.

"They said, 'Oh, so you're going to fake L.A. for New Jersey?' "

" 'No,' " I said. 'I want to shoot it in New Jersey.' "

" 'Oh,' they said, 'shoot the pilot in New Jersey and then bring it back to L.A.? And do a week every five weeks back East for exteriors.' "

"They all looked at me like I was pathetic, obviously dreaming," Mr. Chase said. "It was never going to happen. In the back of my mind I sort of knew it was never going to happen."

Then he went to a meeting at HBO, and the president

of original programming, Chris Albrecht, "says to me, 'So, it's going to be shot in New Jersey. You're going to get New Jersey, right?' "

"And I said, 'Absolutely. You bet.' "

"It's not that Chris loves New Jersey," Mr. Chase said, "but he wanted the show to look distinctive. He felt that if I had bothered to write it that way, it must have some meaning. He said, 'We're going to get New Jersey right,' which led us into a discussion of how the show would look." These days, movies and television series shoot for less in Canada. In recent years, Toronto has been a generic stand-in for Chicago, New York and all suburbs in between. Mr. Chase believes that wouldn't have worked for "The Sopranos."

"I've shot in Toronto," he said. "It isn't New Jersey. It does look different, and that's the end of the story. There's no downtown Jersey City in Toronto. There is no collision of Hispanic, Italian or black around an 1890's brownstone square in Toronto. These are small, unimportant details, perhaps, but not to me."

Not every scene, of course, can be shot in New Jersey. Most of the interiors are filmed at a large studio in Queens because no sound stage in New Jersey is large enough to accommodate the show's needs.

But even in Queens, Mr. Chase has laid down strict guidelines: however expedient it may be, the director is barred from sneaking across the street for a quick storefront or parking-lot shot.

"I just made it a rule," Mr. Chase said. "Let's suppose you have a half day on the stage, and then you have a scene that takes place in a field where they shoot a guy. If you have a parking lot across the street, you change the field to the lot and you don't have to move the entire company across the river. They'll tell you the waterfront looks just like the one in Newark. Baloney. Or, 'I'll show you Italian delis in Queens, and you can't tell the difference.' I'm not interested. Pretty soon that deli in Queens turns into a funeral parlor, which turns into a school, which turns into something else. No way."

Getting authentic means being efficient. That's where the producer, Ilene Landress, and the location staff come in.

"On movies, they are usually shooting two pages a day," Ms. Landress said. "On television, it's seven or eight pages a day. We have eight days to shoot a show."

This means "breaking down the script" into scenes and locations that allow the most efficient use of cast and crew. Can a street-corner encounter, a backyard barbeque and a schoolyard fistfight be filmed in one day?

That depends on the keen eyes of locations scouts with still cameras, and the amiability of homeowners, shopkeepers, school boards, hospital administrators and various municipal overseers.

This also means hoping that potential hosts do not have what Ms. Landress called "unrealistic expectations of what they should receive."

"You hope they're starstruck," she said.

The scouts return, develop their film and the contact sheets are distributed to Ms. Landress, Mr. Chase, the production designer, the director and others. Then they go out and look, again.

Consider the restaurant Vesuvio, owned by Tony Soprano's high school pal Artie. Tony hears that a mob associate has been condemned to a public execution at Vesuvio, the man's favorite hangout. Tony realizes this could wreck Artie's business. He can't figure out a way to get Artie and his wife out of town during the rubout, so he does the next best thing. He asks one of his crew to torch the place.

"We needed to find a restaurant that had some space around it," Ms. Landress said, and she found the very spot in Elizabeth.

"There was a real restaurant on the corner, with a parking lot next to it," she said. "We built a little structure along the street line, with windows and a roof and exploded that."

In another episode, a hapless debtor whom Tony runs down in a Lexus on the lawn of a Paramus office park is persuaded by Soprano pals to repay his loans by embezzling money from his company. The business meeting—a subtle use of geography—takes place on a walkway above the Great Falls, in Paterson.

To call Mr. Chase's pursuit of New Jersey loyalty, love or sentiment would miss the point. Mr. Chase's vision for the series is rooted in something visceral about a place and the creative spirit.

He recalls an earlier experience as a producer of the detective show "The Rockford Files."

"As great a show as it was, the thing that sort of got into my head, was that I felt 'The Rockford Files' was about a place. Despite all the photography that goes on here, where Los Angeles doubles as something else, I felt that the show was happening some place real, not just in its time zone. Trailers on the beach, ritzy houses, driving into the Mexican section. That's why I took the job."

Growing up, Mr. Chase lived in Boonton, briefly, then a garden apartment in Clifton and finally a house his father and grandfather built in North Caldwell in the late 1950's, a two-story stone-and-clapboard colonial.

"As they got established in their life, as all couples do, they sort of moved up," he said of his parents. "They built their dream house. It was based on a plan from House Beautiful, a house in Roslyn, L.I., which we drove out to see."

In 1968, Mr. Chase was married at St. Aloysious Roman Catholic Church, in North Caldwell, "loaded the toaster oven and other junk in the car and drove west" to work in the entertainment business. It would be an overstatement to say that New Jersey haunted him. It is simply where he's from, and it made an impression. Are the wheat fields of Kansas or the arroyos of New Mexico any more significant? Can you go home again? Wrong question. Can you forget where you grew up?

"It probably sounds corny," he said. "You never think about where you live when you're a kid. But when I got to junior high school I began to feel really lucky on some level. I knew I lived someplace special. I knew it was not like any place else."

Speaking of Bloomfield Avenue, the lengthy shopping district that runs through several Essex County communities, Mr. Chase said: "You could be in Iowa City or in West Virginia, it wouldn't make a difference, yet if you climb a tree, you see the New York City skyline. I lived so close to the actual throbbing center of the entire world, yet out here there were fireflies and truck farms."

These are the reminiscences of a baby boomer. Perhaps just a few years older than Tony Soprano (Mr. Chase is evasive about his own age), he is nonetheless part of the great post-war suburban advance, with a sense memory for immigrant experience of his Italian grandparents and the family's physical and emotional migration from city to single-family home on a newly paved street.

When Mr. Chase was a boy, Newark was a thriving city of factories and department stores and a vibrant clash of ethnic neighborhoods. So were Paterson, Jersey City and Elizabeth and the smaller blue-collar towns around them.

Such a one is Kearny, about nine square miles of Hudson County, just east of the Passaic River. One one side, you can see Newark, with a magnificent view of Sacred Heart Cathedral. On the other, Jersey City and Manhattan's skyline.

In between live 35,000 people on streets of multifamily houses separated for the most part only by driveways or alleys. The storefronts still help to identify the immigrant groups: Irish bars, Italian restaurants, Polish sausage shops and, most recently, Portuguese bakeries.

As with much of New Jersey, Kearny was settled by the Dutch, who bought it from the Indians. It underwent several name changes, and was called Harrison (now a separate town) until 1867, when it was renamed for Maj. Gen. Philip Kearny, a Union officer who was killed at Chantilly, Va., in 1862. Belle Grove, the Kearny family estate that resembled a French chateau, was a longtime landmark in the area.

What's so special about Kearny? Everything and nothing. The history and geography lesson would be lost on Tony Soprano or his associates. But the texture of the place is familiar to them, to anyone, who has come to expect realism and authenticity.

The point is: you don't have to go to Little Italy to have a mob sit-down.

All you need, in this case, is Satiale's, a pork store, which occupies center stage in one episode. Satiale's is one of the few exteriors that doesn't really exist. It is an empty double storefront at 101 Kearny Ave., in the southern part of town. But for one episode, it was a thriving Italian meat market, its interior supporting columns painted the colors of the Italian flag. Up the block is a firehouse, and next door is the very real Irish-American Club of Kearny (founded 1933).

The other day, several older men with brogues stood beneath the Irish flag outside and graciously opened the door to their member's-only clubhouse.

Inside, John Kelly, who was born in Glasgow and came to Kearny 38 years ago, was only too happy to talk about the film crew's visit next door.

"It's the one where he meets with the old Jewish guy," Mr. Kelly said, referring to an episode in which an actor dressed as a Hasidic businessman solicits Tony's in putting some muscle on a troublesome son-in-law. "They fixed the place up and put little tables out on the sidewalk."

So they did. A perfectly cozy corner of Kearny on a sunny day, a short walk from St. Ceclia's Roman Catholic Church and just a little farther from the thread and linen companies that brought Scottish and Irish workers here in the last quarter of the 19th century.

Mr. Kelly pointed to the two pool tables and said that they figured in another scene in which F.B.I. agents interrupt crew members and find an arsenal of guns beneath a false table top.

"I watch it every week," Mr. Kelly said enthusiastically. And he added: "Everytime they take the Irish flag down and put up the Italian flag, we get $250."

Members of the production crew for "The Sopranos" received a T-shirt commemorating their 1998 tour of New Jersey, which included these stops.

June 18	Lodi
June 19	Harrison
June 22	Kearny
June 23	Verona, West Orange
July 1	Wayne
July 13	Jersey City
July 15	Paramus
July 24	Oakland
July 29	Madison
Aug. 6	Paterson
Aug. 10	North Caldwell
Aug. 18	Newark
Sep. 1	Bloomfield
Sept. 2	Lincoln Park
Sept. 8	Belleville
Sept. 9	Lyndhurst, North Arlington
Sept. 24	Livingston
Oct. 5	Montclair
Oct. 13	Edison
Oct. 26	Secaucus

—March 7, 1999

ADDICTED TO A MOB FAMILY POTION

by Caryn James

Everyone in therapy talks about mom, but Tony Soprano has a unique family problem. "What do you think?" he asks, outraged at his psychiatrist's suggestion. "My mother tried to have me whacked 'cause I put her in a nursing home?" Well, maybe. In "The Sopranos," HBO's brilliantly nuanced series about a suburban New Jersey mob boss in emotional crisis, the psychiatrist is helping Tony cope with this breakthrough: in the Sopranos' world you truly can't trust your own mother.

When the series began [in January 1999], Mama Livia Soprano was an irascible old woman, addled and comic enough to hit her best friend accidentally with a car. By the time Tony asks that question in the season finale, she has come to resemble a maternal figure with roots in Greek tragedy and even Roman history. Her name should have been a clue from the start. An earlier Livia was the Emperor Claudius's ruthless, scheming grandmother (embodied by Sian Phillips in the mini-series "I

Claudius"). Both Livias are matriarchs who know how to play a bloody family power game.

Livia Soprano's darkening character is simply one strand in the complex web of "The Sopranos," which has become more absorbing and richer at every turn. The series has pulled off an almost impossible feat: it is an ambitious artistic success, the best show of [1999] and many others; it has also become an addictive audience-pleaser, the rare show viewers actually talk and get excited about.

Nancy Marchand, who at first seemed unconvincing as the typical Italian mother, has turned Livia into a singular character. Tony was always more than the easy joke about a modern mobster on Prozac, stressed out by the demands of the job. James Gandolfini plays Tony with a deftness that masks the heft of a tragic hero, with flaws that might make him hateful and a visible soul that evokes sympathy.

Such depth helps explain why "The Sopranos" belongs among the classic miniseries. In its leisurely use of the form, it is strangely like "Brideshead Revisited," "The Singing Detective" and "I, Claudius" (whose historical figures have often been compared to a modern Mafia family). Because the end of the 13-week series was always in sight, it could develop the self-enclosed dramatic tension of a feature film: in the end, would his Uncle Junior take out a hit on Tony in a move to control the family business, or vice versa? Yet it also took the time to create ambiguous characters and the feel of a world through dozens of impeccable small touches.

With its flashy characters and human depths, "The

Sopranos" suggests how thoroughly the Mafia wise guy has become ingrained in American culture, the stuff of both family tragedy and satire. Physically, Tony displays the trappings of a cliche. Overweight with a receding hairline, he wears a jogging suit, gold bracelet and pinky ring. He is a killer. Yet as he frets about his children's education, about whether to put his mother in a nursing home, or about whether an old friend has worn a wire for the F.B.I. and has to be killed, his emotional pain is real. Tony is the mobster as a suburban family man (with bimbo girlfriends on the side) but also as a sensitive 90's guy who wasn't loved enough as a child. Emphatically middle-class, he is like one of your neighbors but with a more dangerous job; that strategy allows viewers to sympathize and experience vicarious danger at once.

David Chase, its creator, is largely responsible for "The Sopranos," but the series' dual essence has been captured most succinctly in an unlikely place: a tag line created by an advertising agency. The ad shows Tony with his mob contacts on one side and his mother, wife and two children on the other; the line reads, "If one family doesn't kill him, the other one will." There is no better statement of the way the two sides of Tony's life converge to give the series its suspense and emotional power.

The earliest episodes only hinted at how rich and tangled its themes would become. The turning point came in Episode 5, when Tony took his daughter, Meadow, to tour New England colleges. Riding in the car, she asks him if he's in the Mafia; at first he denies such a thing exists, then admits that maybe some aspects of his business, ostensibly garbage hauling, are not entirely legal. It is a surprisingly touching conversation, a moment of painful honesty in which the father admits his imperfections and viewers sympathize with his paternal emotions.

Yet while driving Meadow around, he happens to spot a man who once ratted on the mob, then foolishly left the witness protection program. While his daughter is talking to a counselor at Colby College, Tony tracks down the man and garrotes him on camera. Without destroying sympathy for Tony, the series rubs viewers' faces in the fact that he is a murderer.

That on-camera violence, so crucial to the audience's complex, visceral response, is one reason "The Sopranos" could only appear on cable. On network television, his character would surely be sanitized, the violence toned down, the ambiguity cleared up and the entire series diminished. The brilliance of "The Sopranos" depends on the trick of letting us see Tony's worst qualities and getting us to identify with him anyway.

In a later episode, his psychiatrist, Jennifer Melfi (Lorraine Bracco), mentions her patient to her ex-husband, who warns: "Finally, you're going to get beyond psychology with its cheery moral relativism. Finally you're going to get to good and evil, and he's evil." But that voice, from an incidental character, sounds like a disclaimer. It is out of step with the experience of watching "The Sopranos," which is gripping because it is so fraught with moral relativism.

Dr. Melfi remains the weakest link in "The Sopranos," perhaps because she is not truly family. Occasional hints that she will be drawn into Tony's world (he once had a crooked cop tail her on a date) have gone nowhere, and she has remained the ultimate outsider. Viewers, who share Tony's experiences, are more a part of his family than she is.

In fact, feeling inside a Mafia family has become a cultural touchstone. There is some logic behind the coincidence that "The Sopranos" shares a premise with the [1999] hit film "Analyze This," a slight comedy in which Robert De Niro hilariously plays a mobster who, like Tony, suffers panic attacks and ends up at the psychiatrist. Psychiatry is common today, and it is irresistibly funny to imagine a mob boss who is an emotional wreck.

More telling, together these works suggest how deeply Mafia movies have penetrated American culture. In "Analyze This," Mr. De Niro sends up his own classic roles in films like "The Godfather, Part II" and "Goodfellas." In "The Sopranos," Tony's men model themselves on movie mobsters. One man has a car horn that blares out the first bars of "The Godfather" theme; another routinely impersonates Al Pacino as Michael Corleone. Tony's stupidly impulsive nephew, Christopher (Michael Imperioli), tries to write a screenplay about his mob experiences and longs for tabloid fame. Frustrated at his unimportance, Christopher complains that every movie mobster has his own story arc. "Where's my arc?" he says. "I got no identity."

Tony himself is smarter. When he is taken by a neighbor to play golf at a country club, he is bombarded with questions: "How real was 'The Godfather?'" and "Did you ever meet John Gotti?" He may be a killer, but viewers feel for him at that moment; he is wounded at being condescended to and reduced to a cliche.

These 90's mobsters, after all, are a generation removed from the movies that inspired them. "The Sopranos" knowingly hits cultural nerves by responding to the present moment. Meadow reveals the truth about their father's business to her younger brother, Anthony, by showing him a Web site that features pictures of mob bosses. "There's Uncle Jackie!" says Anthony as he spots one of his father's best friends. ("The Sopranos" has its own place on HBO's Web site, which includes a section on the rock-inspired music that is so integral to its realistic feel.)

In the next-to-last episode [in the '99 season,] Tony becomes so depressed he can't get out of bed. Even in this crisis, the series maintains its focus on the credible details of ordinary life. Tony's wife, Carmela, is perfectly played by Edie Falco with a toughened exterior that suggests how she has had to steel herself to her husband's profession. Carmela says, "If you want me I will be at Paramus Mall getting your son a suit for his first formal." One shrewdly drawn plot involves a situation that is absurdly common in real life but rarely discussed. Carmela has a flirtation with a priest, Father Phil, who comes to the house for ziti and movies before safely fleeing back to the church.

The final episode of (the first season) reaches a crescendo of action and intrigue, guilt and retribution. It sets up the story for the next season. And the cumulative weight of the previous weeks adds a delicious resonance to everything Tony says. When he tells a friend whose restaurant he has ordered set on fire, "I didn't burn down your restaurant, I swear on my mother," what exactly does he mean?

—March 25, 1999

A CABLE SHOW NETWORKS TRULY WATCH

by Bill Carter

T he Sopranos" is such a white-hot favorite in the television industry that network executives are trying to figure out how they can copy the breakthrough style of the HBO miniseries and perhaps make up for the mistake several of them made in passing up the show in the first place.

Interest in the cable show has reached such a fever pitch that two networks have even approached its production company to inquire about the possibility of running episodes of "The Sopranos" after they have appeared on HBO.

That seems unlikely, given the show's cable-standard content, which includes nudity, violence and enough florid street language to curl a network censor's toes. But Brad Grey, the executive in charge of Brillstein-Grey Entertainment, which owns "The Sopranos," said yesterday, "The networks are calling now to ask if they can air the shows we've done already."

He would not identify the two networks that made the offer, but he said, "It never reached a serious stage because I just said no." He said he doubted the show could have been edited in a way that wouldn't compromise it creatively.

Besides, it is not as if the broadcast network didn't have a shot at "The Sopranos" the first time around. The show was developed by the drama department of the Fox network in 1996, but it never went anywhere. Mr. Grey said the pilot script written by the show's creator, David Chase, "just came back with a no; we didn't even get any notes from them." Mr. Grey said he then "talked to CBS" about the show, but those conversations led nowhere. And, as usually happens with scripts in Hollywood, word of "The Sopranos" drifted around. One executive who heard about it was David Nevins, the senior vice president of prime-time series at NBC, who said: "I had a shot at it after Fox passed. I thought it was very good. But I couldn't get anyone else interested."

Now the networks are more than interested; they're fascinated.

As Carolyn Ginsburg-Carlson, the senior vice president of comedy for ABC put it, "I love the show; it's one of only three or four shows I make it a point to watch every week."

"The Sopranos" is already a hit by cable standards, scoring ratings higher than any cable channel series in the previous three years. In its Sunday night showing, the show is reaching about 3.7 million viewers, and in its four weekly showings it reaches more than 10 million viewers.

For the people who make television shows for a living, "The Sopranos" is more than an HBO hit; it is a groundbreaker, a show whose influence is likely to be felt throughout the industry in the coming years.

Warren Littlefield, the longtime NBC program chief who is scouting for talent to build his new production company, said the show had prompted the industry to rethink what constitutes "family drama" on television.

"If you look at what network television has done with the family drama, it just made them all dull," Mr. Littlefield said. "We all had blinders on as to how you can present a family on television."

So are networks busy developing shows that will try to embrace the more outrageously creative approach of "The Sopranos?" Not yet, because most of their development was finished before the show went on in January.

Counting itself lucky in terms of timing, CBS does have a Mafia-based drama in development. But its antecedent was the movie "Donnie Brasco," not "The Sopranos." And even broadcast executives disagree on whether the networks could duplicate "The Sopranos" style.

How different is the HBO show from what the networks saw in 1996? Danielle Claman, the Fox drama executive who developed the show (and admits to experiencing a "personal loss" over failing to win support for it at the network) said: "It's 90 percent the same. The show's story is the same, but obviously it is spicier now that it's on HBO."

Mr. Nevins said the original script that he read would have been evaluated by the network standards department. He added: "I don't believe we couldn't do the show on NBC. Content-wise, you could take a little bit out and get it through."

Peter Roth, a former president of Fox Entertainment who is now running the Warner Brothers television stu-

dio, said, "I think 'The Sopranos' is makable for a network. It could play on ABC on Sunday night after 'The Practice.' "

That is not how Chris Albrecht HBO's president of original programming, sees it. "The networks would never have put the show on," he said, adding that what Fox developed as the original script is not the show that so impresses Hollywood now. He noted that HBO was willing to take a risk and allow Mr. Chase to direct the pilot himself. Then there was the crucial decision to allow him to shoot the series on location in New Jersey.

The most important decision HBO made, Mr. Albrecht said—and that point was seconded by every other executive interviewed for this article—was selecting James Gandolfini to play the lead role of Tony Soprano, the gang leader who is so harassed by business and family problems (many of which overlap) that he goes into therapy.

Even one senior NBC executive, speaking on condition of anonymity, said: "If we had done the show, that guy would have never gotten out of the casting room. He is overweight and balding. Somebody would have said: 'He's no TV star. Get somebody sexy.' And we would have messed the whole thing up."

Ms. Claman said Fox had planned to use Anthony LaPaglia as Tony. Even HBO hesitated on Mr. Gandolfini, Mr. Albrecht said, but only because there were two other outstanding auditions for the role, by Steve Van Zandt (best known for his guitar work with Bruce Springsteen), who now plays a Soprano soldier named Silvio, and Michael Rispoli, who played Jackie, the gang leader who died of cancer midway through the season.

Even if a network had taken the risk on Mr. Gandolfini,

Mr. Albrecht said, other decisions would have rendered the show a pale imitation of what is on the air now.

"They would have tried to do New Jersey in L.A.," he said. "And they would have included commercials. You put in commercials and you change the dynamic."

Then there is the money. "They would try to make this for $1.6 million an episode," Mr. Albrecht said. "We're spending $300,000 to $400,000 more."

Mr. Littlefield is one executive from the network side who agreed that "The Sopranos" needed all the freedom that HBO provides. "You can't just take that content and language out," he said. "The content is part of that overall gestalt; it's part of what surprises you. Those surprises are one reason you don't want to miss any episode."

Mr. Albrecht would like nothing better than to be able to provide more episodes of "The Sopranos" for its rabid fans. He fears breaking the show's powerful momentum. But new episodes will not be back until January 2000. In July, HBO will repeat the first batch of 13. And HBO has asked Mr. Chase to try to do more than 13 [for the second season]. "I'm hoping for 15 or 16," Mr. Albrecht said.

[In the meantime] the rest of the television business will study what executives have seen so far and try to take away some lessons.

"The lesson is: there's reward in keeping an audience guessing, keeping them on their toes," Mr. Nevins said.

Mr. Littlefield said: "I think what it's telling us is that we've got to think differently when we create shows. But it also reminds us that the world we live in is both diverse and really outrageous."

—March 25, 1999

THE SON WHO CREATED A HIT, 'THE SOPRANOS'

by Alex Witchel

David Chase, the creator of the HBO phenomenon "The Sopranos," picked me up at noon. We were driving to Elizabeth, N.J., for lunch at Manolo's, a restaurant he used as a location in the series—one that the mobster Tony Soprano torches.

"Do you really want to go to New Jersey?" Mr. Chase asked uneasily.

"Well, yes, I guess so," I said, a bit thrown. It had taken weeks of phone calls to arrange this meeting, since Mr. Chase is more than a little press-shy. "I thought you wanted to go to New Jersey."

"I didn't want to go," he insisted.

"You didn't?" I asked.

"No, I thought you did."

"Well, we don't have to," I said, trying desperately to think of an alternative.

He looked surprised. "Oh, I don't care if we go."

At that moment I realized there would be no need to

speak to Nancy Marchand, who plays Livia Soprano, mob mother from hell. I had just seen the real thing.

Mr. Chase has created a cast of characters for his smash hit show who are completely idiosyncratic and unforgettable. But it is Livia—a mother so angry at her son for moving her to a nursing home that she helps put a hit out on him—who is a little more unforgettable than the rest. She is, of course, inspired in part by Mr. Chase's own mother, Norma, who died five years ago at the age of 34.

"She was, uh, a complete original," Mr. Chase said, seated at a corner table at Manolo's. He laughed uneasily, looking down at the tablecloth. "She had this incredible thing where she was very easily offended, yet there was never a person on earth who censored herself less. The way she acted was very sad. As she got older, she started insulting more and more people, taking umbrage at things they said and cutting herself off from the world. At a time when she was getting older and people die or get sick anyway, she was shrinking her circle by her own doing. It was very odd."

Mr. Chase said his parents had "married pretty late, in their early 30's." His father, Henry, was born in Providence, R.I., his mother in Newark, though both sets of parents came from Italy. Mr. Chase is an only child and neither of his parents was Roman Catholic: his father was Baptist; his mother, the 10th of 11 children, was reared by a "socialist atheist" father who loved opera and named some of his daughters after his favorites, including Norma and her sister Livia.

Mr. Chase was born in Mount Vernon, N.Y., but he won't say when. He worries about revealing his age in youth-obsessed Hollywood, though he offers "50-ish" as an estimate. He will also not give his daughter's name or where she will attend college. He says it was his paternal grandmother who changed the family name from DeCesare to Chase, but he won't say why. "It was a situation of l'amour fou" is as far as he'll go, worried that relatives will get angry if he divulges more.

His mother was a worrier, too, he said. "She worried about cancer, car accidents, criminals breaking into the house. And my father did get cancer. So did all her sisters."

What did Norma Chase make of her only child, a graduate of New York University who earned a master's in film from Stanford University and won Emmy Awards for his writing and directing of the hit series "I'll Fly Away" and "Northern Exposure"?

He grimaced toward the tablecloth and closed his eyes, something he did often. He seemed to keep hoping that when he finally opened them, I would have disappeared.

"I don't know," he said. "I was so far out of her world. My first directing job was an episode of 'Alfred Hitchcock Presents,' and I called to tell her and she said, 'Really? Did they accept it?' " For as many times as he has obviously told this story, he still gasps with the disbelief of a hurt child.

" 'I don't cater to anybody,' she used to say. But there was a kind of self-awareness of what she was doing. Sometimes I would think: 'She's doing performance art. It's a character she's made up.' She was aware sometimes that she was being outrageous and provocative."

When Mr. Chase was 5, the family moved from Mount

Vernon to Clifton, N.J., where Mr. Chase got A's in every-thing except deportment, in which he got F's. "I was out of my chair, talking a lot," he said. "I was always jig-gling." Even now, sitting at the table, his hand drums its edge, then fools incessantly with a straw wrapper. When he was in seventh grade, the family moved to North Caldwell, N.J. His father owned a hardware store in Verona, and Mr. Chase worked there on Saturdays when he was growing up.

"I hated doing it, naturally," he said. He made another grimace. "My father had quit his job as an engineer in the early 50's and opened this Main Street hardware store right when places like E. J. Korvette were just beginning. It never really took off."

His mother always worked, Mr. Chase said. For the most part, she spent her career with the telephone com-pany, proofreading directories. He half smiled. "She had the ability to be in both places at the same time," he said. "She would say 'I hate it' and later say 'I didn't say I hate it; I don't know where you got that from.' " Which is very much like Livia Soprano, who Mr. Chase says wields "the tyranny of the weak."

"They orchestrate a lot of disturbance and require a lot of coddling and special attention just to get them to stop," he said. "All anyone wants to do is give them what they want."

No one is all bad, of course. What is his fondest mem-ory of his mother? "I have lots of them," he said. "Once she got me some Ray Charles records for Christmas, which was not her kind of music at all. I knew she'd got-ten them and where she had hidden them and one night I was drinking at my house with friends. I got them out and played them. I felt so warm and appreciative. And she didn't yell."

Mr. Chase says that his family was not involved in the Mafia, though he adds, "I was crazy about the Mafia since I was a kid." Watching "The Million Dollar Movie" helped. Even now, he can—and does—recite most of "Public Enemy" complete with a description of camera angles. "It blew my mind. It hooked me. I don't know why, but it did."

It seems completely out of character that Mr. Chase has lived in Los Angeles for the last 28 years. He has no tan, no real color in his face at all. He is balding and his hair is gray. And rather than preening about his new-found success, he doubts his good fortune, scared some-how that it will be taken away. He is sure he is about to contract "a horrible illness."

Is it time to go back into therapy? He shrugged. The character of Dr. Jennifer Melfi (Lorraine Bracco) reflects Mr. Chase's own experience with a female therapist, though he says he saw "three or four men before that and they all did me some good." One heavy-breathing specu-lation about "The Sopranos" is that Tony (James Gandolfini), who is treated by Dr. Melfi, will have an affair with her. Though Mr. Chase is careful not to divulge too much of what will happen [in the second] season, his response to this is definite.

"Ludicrous," he fumed. "The hiding and shame is not what the show's about. And the therapy would be ruined."

"The Sopranos" goes back into production in July [of 1999], and 13 new episodes go on the air in January [2000]. The show is shot on location in New Jersey, and at the Silvercup Studios in Astoria, Queens. It is staff written, meaning Mr. Chase and three or four other writers work together on "beating out stories." Mr. Chase directs some episodes; he also casts, edits and scores them.

"The second year was never planned out," he said. When HBO rescued the series, it had been rejected by the networks and Mr. Chase couldn't see past the first season. "What concerns me most now is the noise from the outside world," he said. "Can we keep this up? Last year my feeling was only 'we have nothing to lose.' "

As for how many more seasons fans can hope for, Mr. Chase is noncommittal. "Given the life that Tony's in, it can't go on forever," he said. "Something has to happen."

For now, though, he says he loves writing for this cast. "As a writer I usually start off in a defended position. For example, I put three dots at the end of a sentence so it will trail off and then the actor reading it ends the sentence. I used to think actors were only there to ruin everything. They terrified me. I had a sense with actors that they have all the fun, that they're less responsible than the rest of us. It made me jealous. I came to it late, but I see now that they're the best part of it."

As for directing, Mr. Chase said: "It terrifies me. That first time-directed, the Alfred Hitchcock show, I was so scared that the night before I had thoughts of going to the Greyhound station and leaving L.A. It felt like the time I was 11 and sprained my ankle on a camping trip and went to visit my grandmother in Mount Vernon. And my aunt had just had a baby and for some reason I wanted to carry him. My ankle gave out and I dropped the baby. I ran out of the house screaming. Directing felt like that. I felt lame with the whole thing."

"I've always been anxious, fearful, competitive, envious and angry," he went on matter-of-factly, talking about his drive to succeed. "When I'm on the set, though, I don't freak out. I say to myself, 'You know what, this looks like life, but it's not. Whatever happens here isn't going to kill you.' " The grimace finally slid into a smile. "That's about the best I can do."

—June 6, 1999

FROM THE HUMBLE MINI-SERIES COMES THE MAGNIFICENT MEGAMOVIE

by Vincent Canby

Movies and television have been feeding off each other for years, each trying to capture whatever part of the mass audience is the other's territory. In this age of political strategy dictated by public opinion poll, movies and television behave like a pair of rival party candidates for the same office: each side quietly adopts policies that differ from the other's only in degree, rarely in substance.

When innovative thinking is discouraged, choices dwindle in art as well as politics. Movies imitate television as television imitates movies that imitate television. While the screens in so-called home entertainment centers are getting bigger and bigger, movie theater audiences, with increasing frequency, carry on as if at home, talking, swilling their sodas and chomping junk food labeled lite.

And why not?

Today's audiences have been conditioned. A theater is simply a first-run outlet for material that will be seen again in the living room. Pop theatrical movies and television dramas are essentially the same: a dependence on close-ups, on shock effects and on pacing of narratives to bridge commercial interruptions, whether the interruptions exist now or are to be inserted later.

When there are exceptions, they usually come from independent and foreign filmmakers, seldom from television sources.

Thus, the effect is tonic when something turns up as singular as "The Sopranos," HBO's 13-episode, nearly 13-hour melodramatic comedy, created by the seriously talented David Chase. It is also an event that prompts an examination of what our films and our television series have become and what their possibilities are, given the circumstances in which they are produced and the contexts in which they are seen.

"The Sopranos" did not emerge whole and complete like a sonnet from a single artist working in splendid isolation. Rather, it came out of the same rough-and-tumble process by which teams of collaborators have traditionally put together everything from soap operas, police and hospital dramas and sitcoms to shows as idiosyncratic as Roseanne's and Fraiser's.

It's not too much, I think, to compare "The Sopranos" to such seminal works as "Berlin Alexanderplatz" (1980), Rainer Werner Fassbinder's 15 1/2-hour adaptation of Alfred Doblin's epic 1929 German novel, and "The Singing Detective" (1988), the tumultuous six-hour British production based on Dennis Potter's original script about the physical and moral redemption of an overly imaginative sinner with a skin condition. Both were created to be seen as television mini-series, which they were.

"The Sopranos," shown as what was, in effect, a mini-series, was produced in the hope that it would become a continuing HBO series if successful, which it was. Thirteen new episodes have already been filmed, to be broadcast starting in January [2000].

"Berlin Alexanderplatz," "The Singing Detective" and "The Sopranos" are something more than mini-series. Packed with characters and events of Dickensian dimension and color, their time and place observed with satiric exactitude, each has the kind of cohesive dramatic arc that defines a work complete unto itself. No matter what they are labeled or what they become, they are not open-ended series, or even mini-series.

They are megamovies.

That is, they are films on a scale imagined by the big-thinking, obsessive, fatally unrealistic Erich von Stroheim when, in 1924, he shot "Greed," virtually a page-by-page adaptation of Frank Norris's Zola-esque novel, "McTeague." Stroheim intended it to be an exemplar of cinematic realism.

He also imagined audiences with cast-iron constitutions. His first cut ran nine and a half hours. He later reduced the running time to something less than five hours. Yet before "Greed" was sent out to theaters, the film had been taken away from him and others had removed more than three-quarters of the master's original material.

In 1950, after being persuaded to look at the mutilated final version in the archives of the French Cinematheque in Paris, Stroheim is reported to have said: "This was like an exhumation for me. In a tiny coffin I found a lot of dust, a terrible smell, a little backbone and shoulder bone."

Had television and the mini-series format been available 75 years ago, it is possible that Stroheim would have been spared his humiliation. "Greed" might have survived in something resembling the director's version. It could have been one of history's first megamovies.

Now we have mini-series, though few of these have the tight focus and consistency of tone associated with the megamovies I've mentioned. The English adaptation of Jane Austen's "Pride and Prejudice" qualifies. The "Brideshead Revisited" mini-series might qualify, even if, for me, anyway, it has the mournful expression and rouged cheeks of something embalmed. Unlike "Berlin Alexanderplatz," "The Singing Detective" and "The Sopranos," "Brideshead" never achieves its own identity. This may be because the novel, which it recreates with solemnity, itself seems a romantic and pious literary exercise compared with Waugh's comic masterpieces "Decline and Fall," "Vile Bodies" and "A Handful of Dust."

"The Sopranos," about the world of a New Jersey Mafia kingpin who seeks the help of a psychiatrist after suffering acute anxiety attacks, is no spinoff of "The Godfather" films or any kind of variation on the Robert De Niro-Billy Crystal comedy, "Analyze This." It's a stunning original about a most particular slice of American life, a panoramic picture that is, by turns, wise, brutal, funny and hair-raising, and of significance to the society just beyond its immediate view.

Equally important is the way "The Sopranos" calls to mind the collaborative process that was accepted in Hollywood before every director considered himself an "auteur," to give the director the status of artist and largely to ignore the collaborators. In truth, the term auteur, as it was used by Francois Truffaut and his colleagues in the New Wave of French filmmakers and critics in the 1950's, was reserved for those directors of pronounced personal style and vision. In recent decades, though, it has become simply a fancy way to identify anyone who manages to receive a credit as a director.

The manner in which "The Sopranos" came together sounds initially less like Truffaut's now-classical auteurism than the old days at MGM or Warner Brothers or 20th Century Fox. This would cover the Hollywood studio system from the 1930's into the 1950's, when a production chief like Louis B. Mayer, Jack L. Warner or Darryl F. Zanuck vetted every film on his lot, changed directors at will, recut films to his tastes and secretly assigned writers to rewrite scripts not yet completed by the original writers.

No less than 11 directors receive credit for "The Sopranos" (two of whom each directed two segments), as well as eight writers (who sometimes wrote alone, sometimes in pairs or in threes) and two different directors of photography.

As the man who conceived the project and who, as the executive producer, kept its large team in harness, Mr. Chase is the show's undisputed auteur. He wrote and directed the first episode, take solo writing credit for another and collaborated on scripts for two others.

Though "The Sopranos" received 16 Emmy nominations, the members of the Academy of Television Arts and Sciences, a traditional base for broadcast (as opposed to cable) television, finally gave the show only two awards. James Manos Jr. and Mr. Chase shared an award for the

script of the fifth episode. Edie Falco was voted best actress in a drama for her performance as Carmela Soprano, the Mafia boss's wife, a loving, worried, common-sensical woman who aspires to respectability.

The production was budgeted to come in at $1.9 million to $2 million per episode, which would have made the total cost in the neighborhood of $26 million. That is small change by standards in Hollywood, where $26 million is not an outrageous budget for a comparatively plain, contemporary two-hour movie. By those same standards, "The Sopranos," as a nearly 13-hour feature film, might have cost $169 million, without even trying to sink the "Titanic."

In describing the production of "The Sopranos," Mr. Chase makes it sound like the process by which a platoon of great comedy writers, ruled by Sid Caesar, put together the seminal Caesar shows of the 1950's. According to Mr. Chase, the writers of each "Sopranos" segment would meet to discuss ideas, sometimes augmented by suggestions from the other writers. Everybody chimed in. Each segment was shot fast—eight days—though they often went into overtime. There was a good deal of reshooting and a certain number of disagreements. That is, everything was perfectly normal.

Mr. Chase's background is in television, commercial and cable, where his credits as a producer, writer and director include "The Rockford Files," "I'll Fly Away" and "Northern Exposure." Nothing he had done before, though, was preparation for the achievement of "The Sopranos." Here is the comic, frequently tortured journey toward self-awareness of Tony Soprano, affluent suburban family man, loyal son to a brutish mother, loyal

Mafia member, extortionist and unhesitating executioner.

His immediate problem as he sees it: his business as a "waste disposal consultant" is "trending downward." More deep rooted are moral crises. Tony is a guy who is moved to scary (to him), inexplicable tears when he remembers a family of migrating ducks that had made an extended stopover in his expensive swimming pool, then suddenly abandoned the pool to continue the flight north.

The seamlessness of the direction, the writing, the photography (here is one show in which every close-up has a point and the camera never loses sight of physical context) is matched in the ensemble performances by the breathtaking cast.

Most notable: James Gandolfini (the heavy-lidded Tony, an assassin with sweet instincts he can't comprehend, a nascent beer belly and a short fuse), the splendid Ms. Falco, Lorraine Bracco (Tony's psychiatrist, whose treatment of her patient results in problems for both that Freud never dreamed of), Dominic Chianese (Tony's aging uncle and immediate mob superior, who is nearly undone by his longtime mistress) and Michael Imperioli (Tony's raging nephew, who aspires to be both a "made" man of the mob and a screenwriter). Dominating every scene she is in is Nancy Marchand as Tony's mother, a tough, emotionally stingy woman who wears a frown as her umbrella. It is she who instigates the kind of revenge on a son (he doesn't love her enough) to which only a mob widow and mother has access.

I saw "The Sopranos" not as it was initially broadcast at the rate of one segment per week, but at my own pace on cassettes supplied by HBO. Once I watched four together, another time three, but always at least two. This gives the critic an edge over the general public. Momentum builds. Small but important details that might otherwise be forgotten from one week to the next, or simply overlooked while one is attending to the plot, remain vivid.

Yet such privileged viewing also has the potential to create the sort of intimacy that makes it easier to spot lapses in continuity, contradictions within characters and a too-ready reliance on story formulas. "The Sopranos" not only survives such close inspection, but also benefits from it. A series like "Law and Order" does not. If cassettes are one way to establish that intimate contact, syndication is another.

How we respond to television fare depends on the manner in which we see it. Commercial-free premium cable channels, as good as they are, still lock one into someone else's scheduling. Cassettes are ideal, but there aren't that many mini-series or megamovies at the corner video shop.

Though the networks still dominate the television market, their audiences are dwindling. More and more people are apparently realizing that so-called free television demands too high a price: that we surrender an ever-increasing proportion of our attention to the contemplation of commercials. Since the rules were changed during the Reagan years, broadcasters can stuff any program with as many commercials as they can get away with. Only children's programs are regulated.

There are ways to avoid commercials, of course—riding the remote, going to the fridge—but in the long run commercials win: it's just too much trouble to run away.

In our society we celebrate advertising as an art form, which it may be. Advertising also helps to keep the economy going. Yet no child grows up today without being aware of the gulf between the real world and the world as seen in television commercials and in much of the entertainment they support. Isn't it possible the resulting skepticism eventually can evolve into something more pernicious: an unfocused, closeted cynicism that explodes in violence of no easily recognized motivation?

Such are the thoughts suggested by a show as fresh and provocative as "The Sopranos," which has nothing to do with advertising but a lot to do with the temper of American life, especially with the hypocrisies that go unrecognized.

At one point, Tony tries to persuade Meadow, his teen-age daughter, that, although he has mob connections, her life is no different from those of the doctor's children who live next door. Her reply: "Did the Cusamano kids ever find $50,000 in Krugerrands and a .45 automatic while hunting for Easter eggs?"

There is a difference. Meadow knows it. So does Tony. "The Sopranos," which plays as a dark comedy, possesses a tragic conscience.

—October 31, 1999

REHABILITATING HER IMAGE

by Ginia Bellafante

When some aspiring actresses envision their own stardom, they think of time spent writing gushy notes to their good friend Tom Ford, thanking him for all those feathered jeans and python stilettos he keeps sending over, no bill enclosed.

During the decade-plus she struggled to make it in show business, Edie Falco was never one to harbor those fantasies. Fashion simply wasn't something Ms. Falco, the star of "The Sopranos," the HBO series, thought much about. For years she happily made do with unfeathered jeans and discarded clothes from the movies on which a friend, Eric Mendelsohn, assisted the costume designers. Once, Mr. Mendelsohn recalled, he gave Ms. Falco items from a film in which the lead character, named Dottie, just wore things with dots. "For a long time, Edie only wore dots," Mr. Mendelsohn said. Now a director, he cast Ms. Falco in the title role of his first feature, "Judy Berlin," released in February [2000].

But this kind of ad hoc approach to dressing doesn't

work once you are finally famous, as Ms. Falco is learning. Shortly after a television show declared her one of the worst-dressed guests at the Emmys in September[1999]— an event in which she won the best-actress award for her portrayal of Carmela Soprano, the mob wife with social aspirations—HBO provided Ms. Falco with the services of a stylist, Toni Fusco, and a $20,000 budget to help the actress refurbish her image.

From her apartment in Manhattan last week, Ms. Falco said she was humiliated when she discovered from friends that panelists on Melissa and Joan River's post-Emmy show had found her seemingly innocuous Pamela Dennis skirt and halter top so offensive. "It's actually a big deal for me to get dressed like a grown-up," she explained. "I thought I looked good."

"I was embarrassed at how embarrassed I was," she said.

Ms. Falco dealt with her shame by joking to all her "Sopranos" colleagues about her worst-dressed status, hoping she'd be the first to tell them. (Everyone, as it turns out, already knew.) Ms. Falco began asking a "Sopranos" costume designer for fashion advice, and soon enough Ms. Fusco was called by the network's talent-relations office to help the "Sopranos" star do some shopping. (A spokeswoman for HBO said she couldn't comment on the matter.)

"I thought she looked beautiful at the Emmys," Ms. Fusco said. "I felt so bad for her." On their major shopping outing, Ms. Fusco took the actress to DKNY (Ms. Falco's suggestion), Barney's New York, Bergdorf Goodman and Manolo Blahnik (the stylist's choices). Ms.

Falco bought a pantsuit, a handkerchief skirt, some cashmere sweaters and a few pairs of pumps. But bleeding HBO dry she is not. The actress's total purchases came to about $4,000.

—November 16, 1999

THE SOPRANOS

by Ralph Blumenthal

His favorite uncle tried to have him whacked, his terrified shrink skipped town, his best friend may have betrayed him, and his malevolent mother, whom he was about to suffocate with a pillow, has just had a stroke. And you think *you* have problems?

With that and lots of other baggage, Tony Soprano and his gang of endearing mob misfits and dysfunctional kin embark on a second season of the runaway hit series *The Sopranos* on HBO. Last year's 13 episodes about an existentialist New Jersey Mafia boss in training to become a human being became the most lionized television phenomenon of 1999, winning legions of new customers for HBO and garnering 16 Emmy nominations but in the end taking away only two awards. (Maybe the Emmy voters never heard what happens to people who rob the mob.)

Still, the family that preys together stays together, and so *The Sopranos*—with James Gandolfini as Tony, the lout with doubts and a human heart; Edie Falco as his sage and forgiving wife, Carmela; and Lorraine Bracco as Tony's ultra-professional yet enigmatically tempting psychiatrist, Dr. Melfi—are back with 13 new episodes that could be the prelude, its producers say, to a third season and perhaps more.

"The new episodes prove the show has room to grow," said Brad Grey, the executive producer who teamed up more than three years ago with David Chase, a writer, to create the series out of Mr. Chase's primordial issues with his own difficult mother.

Just don't ask them what's in store this season. They could tell you. But then they'd have to kill you.

HBO has given out some clues, however, and inevitably, with reporters invited to watch tapings at the Silvercup Studios in Long Island City, Queens, other tidbits have been leaking for weeks.

It is known, for example, that Tony Soprano visits Naples. His long-estranged older sister, Janice (played by Aida Turturro), driven away by their crafty beast of a mother, Livia (Nancy Marchand), returns home. After Jackie Aprile (Michael Rispoli), the acting boss of the Soprano family, died of cancer in Episode 4 last year, his menacing brother Richie (David Proval) now shows up, boding ill for Soprano family harmony. Dr. Melfi gets analyzed by *her* shrink, played by the director Peter Bogdanovich. Uncle Junior (Dominic Chianese), who put out the botched hit on his nephew Tony and then was arrested in an FBI sweep, gets out of jail. Into Tony's checkered love life comes an old flame, played by the stage actress Mary Louise Wilson.

In another innovation this season, Michael Imperioli, who plays Christopher, Tony's violently unstable nephew and a would-be screenwriter, makes the unusual transition to a writer of one of the episodes. "I always used to write in my basement," said Mr. Imperioli, who is no neophyte: he was co-writer of *Summer of Sam*, the Spike Lee movie about the paranoia set off by the serial killer David Berkowitz.

One other confidence can be revealed, as one of the season's directors, Tim Van Patten, imparted to this reporter: "People get whacked."

Just don't ask who. And don't ask what happened to Big Pussy Bompensero (Vincent Pastore), Tony's beloved sidekick and then suspected rat who disappeared mysteriously in Episode 11.

Last season's finale provided a powerful springboard into the new season. Here's how viewers left the Sopranos in April (and in subsequent reruns):

After conspiring with her pet brother-in-law, Uncle Junior, to have Tony, her own son, murdered out of pique that he might be complaining to his psychiatrist about her, Livia suffers a convenient memory loss. When Tony does complain to Dr. Melfi about his mother, and the shrink sympathizes with him, Tony leaps at her viciously: "That's my mother we're talking about!" They make up, but after the FBI rounds up Uncle Junior and 15 other members of the family (but not Tony), Dr. Melfi is spooked enough to take Tony's advice and flee town, leaving Tony shrinkless.

Feeling besieged on all sides and suffering existential angst ("What kind of person can I be when his own mother wants him dead?") Tony rebuffs FBI efforts to turn him into an informant. He goes to the hospital determined to take care of his mother once and for all—

he ominously snatches a pillow on the way to her room—just as she is wheeled out in the throes of an apparent seizure. But, under her oxygen mask, why is she smiling?

It all ends on a poignant note, with Tony, Carmela and their two untamed children, Meadow and Anthony Jr. (Jamie Lynn Sigler and Robert Iler), finding refuge from a storm (metaphor alert!) in a friend's restaurant, where two of Tony's underlings, Paulie Walnuts and Silvio Dante (Tony Sirico and Steven Van Zandt) privately predict his imminent recrowning as family boss. Tony raises a glass to his brood: "Someday soon you'll have families of your own, and if you're lucky you'll remember the little moments like this that were good."

Whether the new episodes will meet the high expectations raised by the first 13 will have to be seen, but if they do—and Mr. Chase and many of the same writers and directors worked on the new season for Brillstein-Grey Entertainment—*The Sopranos* is likely to be a prime contender again at this summer's Emmy Awards. Last year Ms. Falco won for best actress and Mr. Chase for best writing of a drama series, but other series nominees, including Mr. Gandolfini, were ignored, to the consternation of many critics who saw the results as evidence of the networks' reluctance to accept cable television channels as full industry partners.

If the show's success is widely attributed to the superior writing and the inspired casting of a universe of miscreants with human foibles, the actors, directors and producers have no quarrel with that. In fact, a number of them said in recent interviews, the company has bonded to an extraordinary degree. "It feels at times like we've been together in a past life," said Ms. Falco of her on-screen marriage to Mr. Gandolfini. "Our jaws drop at how comfortable we are with each other."

Ms. Bracco, who came up with the idea of transporting the cast to the Emmys last year all together in a bus, said, "There's something so fabulous about loving all the cast and crew." Where it became artistically dicey, she said, was in the highly charged sexuality Tony brings to his sessions with Dr. Melfi, who, Ms. Bracco said, struggles to remain professionally aloof, to the point of wearing her hair shorter and her skirts longer.

"He's very attracted to me, I know," she said. "I have to be very careful. If I gave Mr. Soprano an inkling of interest, he would eat me up and spit me out."

So where will it end? Is *The Sopranos* destined to continue season after season into the television record books? Mr. Chase won't rule it out, but he's cautious. "From my standpoint," he said, "there is a point at which a television series becomes a walking dead parody of itself. I hope we see it and shoot ourselves in the head first."

—January 9, 2000

HE ENGINEERED A MOB HIT, AND NOW IT'S TIME TO PAY UP

by Bill Carter

If there is one thing a soprano should know, it's how to pull off an encore.

But for David Chase, the maestro behind "The Sopranos," the HBO mob opera that became the most wildly celebrated show of turn-of-the-century American television, the prospect of an encore to last season's critical and commercial triumph is bringing with it an almost crushing burden of extravagant expectations.

"I have back problems such that I can't walk," Mr. Chase said, forcing a laugh as he reeled off a litany of his recent physical woes. "I have lip problems, problems with my chest wall. I shouldn't say it's related to the pressure, but I think so. I really do."

The return of "The Sopranos" to HBO this coming Sunday night at 9 is surely the most eagerly awaited second season of a television series in recent years. The first 13 episodes last year were called everything from the best show of the year to the best of the decade to even the best television show ever. HBO has waged a promotional campaign that has underscored that praise, capitalized it, put it in italics and shouted it from the rooftops.

Brad Grey, who with Mr. Chase is an executive producer of the show, said "You see everything HBO is doing and, to be honest, you enjoy it in one sense. But I try to remind everyone: Let's all remember, we're doing a television show here."

Mr. Chase is a veteran television writer who has worked on such series as "The Rockford Files" and "Northern Exposure." He created "The Sopranos" from his own intensely personal vision after years of trying to sell the story of Tony Soprano, a strikingly human northern New Jersey mobster, and his dysfunctional families, personal and professional, to movies and then to television networks. He admitted he had no inkling when he wrapped up the initial batch of episodes last January that he would soon be at the center of a success so phenomenal he would begin receiving fan letters from people like Stephen King and signed guitars from Elvis Costello.

"I mean, this is beyond my wildest dreams," Mr. Chase said in an interview at the Stanhope Hotel near his home in Manhattan. "Last year we'd be out there shooting, myself and the cast, and we'd say to ourselves, Who's going to watch this? We were having a really good time doing it. And I guess it's the Puritan ethic: if you're really enjoying yourself, you're going to be punished."

Instead, of course, Mr. Chase and his actors, James Gandolfini, who plays Tony; Edie Falco, who plays his wife, Carmela; Nancy Marchand, who plays his conniving mother, Livia; and many of the others were swept away in a wave of adulation, including Emmys for Mr. Chase (writing) and for Ms. Falco (leading actress in a drama series).

Now comes the hard part. Doing it again.

"When I sat down to start the second season I did have the feeling, now what am I going to do?" Mr. Chase said. "And you're aware there's a thing called a sophomore slump." The pressure, he said, began to kick in fully last April, when the show became the subject of a special event put on by the Museum of Television and Radio in Los Angeles. It was mobbed with fans from the entertainment industry.

"I could sit here and say, listen, I'm an artist, we artists do things for ourselves. It's really about expressing ourselves and pleasing ourselves," Mr. Chase said. "And there's a certain truth to that. I think you have to be somewhat true to your vision. Otherwise you'd go crazy chasing something all the time.

"But we're social animals. We're like dogs. If the other dogs turn on you, it's going to hurt. You're going to feel bad. You don't want the rest of the pack to turn on you, the pack that first embraced you. I'd be kidding you to say it was anything else."

Mr. Chase said he and his team of writers started discussions about framing a second season as far back as last February. The biggest problem they faced, he said, was purely mechanical: having closed year one with Tony's mother having organized an attempt on his life, and the arrest of his other main antagonist, Uncle Junior, "Suddenly Tony and his mother are not speaking," Mr. Chase said. "And Uncle Junior's not there. All the things you rely on to get through a writers' meeting to be able to go home—'So then he talks to his mother and they have a fight about X'—you don't have those anymore."

There was no specific plan to write the season finale last year with some kind of dangling plot points, Mr. Chase said. "We kept thinking we didn't know there'd be a next season. We've got to shoot our best shot. We'll have to sacrifice whatever second season there is to the first, because the first is all we have. So there was some stuff to work out."

The solutions include new characters, like Tony's long-lost sister, Janice, an exile from the counterculture (whose commune name is the Hindu goddess Parvati), and a threatening mobster just out of the pen, Richie Aprile. Mr. Chase said his biggest problem remained Tony's relationship with his mother, one reason Tony was in therapy all last season.

Not only is it difficult to find a way to bring Tony and Livia back even into the same room, he said, but, "coming off the events of last year, things happened to Tony to make him a more volatile person."

While the violence quotient, which Mr. Chase said the series had consciously tried to keep under control last season, may seem slightly elevated as the season begins, he added, "It's not that we just want to pump it up and put more violence in it but that Tony has a lot more rage."

Tony's rage was a factor in the one instance last season when the show ran into some opposition from HBO, Mr. Chase said. In the now-memorable episode where Tony takes his daughter Meadow on a college-shopping trip to Maine and encounters a former gang member who turned state's evidence, HBO executives vocally protested its climax, where Tony kills his despised former colleague with his bare hands.

"HBO said you can't do this," Mr. Chase said. "You've built up the most interesting protagonist on television in the past 25 years, and now you're just going to lose it. There was a big discussion." He said he argued that to have Tony not kill "a rat" would be so counter to his character "that we'd lose viewers."

As it turned out, the episode was almost too good for Mr. Chase. "I saw it and said: Why did we do this for a TV series? This would be such a great independent movie."

HBO's decision to allow Tony to be seen committing brutal murder underscored Mr. Chase's conviction that "The Sopranos" could have achieved this level of success only on an outlet like HBO.

Originally, Mr. Grey, whose studio, now called Basic Entertainment, owned the right to the show, placed it at the Fox network. After a pilot script, the network passed on making the series, as did CBS and ABC. Mr. Grey says: "The truth is I was wrong. You could never have made this at Fox or any other network."

Mr. Chase said that restrictions on the wholesale vulgarity that contributes so significantly to the show's verisimilitude would have been the least of the problems at a network. "I just know they would have tried to make it that, on the side, he's helping the F.B.I. find the guys who blew up the World Trade Center. That claptrap. That would have been horrible."

Thirteen new episodes are in the final stages of produciton. HBO has already made it clear it wants more, and Mr. Chase said he has committed verbally to another season. "We'll start meeting again in February, blocking out stories." After that, he said, there are a "bunch of clauses" for further seasons.

"I love this," Mr. Chase said. "Who would let go of this?"

It is a big change, he admitted, after having chafed for much of his career at being limited mainly to television. "All my life I wanted to do movies. I just resented every moment I spent in television. But I would up in TV and it provided a good living and I was very fortunate that I worked on really good shows.

"But for me it was always cinema, cinema, cinema. Now this has been so good. Where am I ever going to go where it's going to be this good again?"

—January 11, 2000

HBO WANTS TO MAKE SURE YOU NOTICE

by Bill Carter

Spike Lee was there; so were Christopher Walken and Aiden Quinn and Stephen King and the present and former police commissioners of the city of New York. The party at Roseland on Wednesday night was the biggest ever given by HBO, no stranger to lavish premiere parties.

But then HBO has never before had anything quite as big as "The Sopranos" to promote.

The cable channel had planned on about 1,000 guests; about 1,800 showed up for the party and screening of two episodes in the new season. The Ziegfield theater could not contain the crowd, so HBO bused the latecomers to its headquarters on Avenue of the Americas. On the way they may have glimpsed one of the many "Sopranos" billboards dotting the city, or at least seen a city bus go by with the cast glaring out in full menace just above the message, "Family: Redefined."

Had some taken the subway, there's a chance they could have ridden in one of the cars "fully branded"—as

HBO's top marketing executive put it—with "Sopranos" advertising: nothing but black-and-white images of the cast.

It is all part of what Eric Kessler, the executive vice president for marketing at HBO, called a campaign "comparable to the biggest thing we've ever done." And why not, he added, "We're talking about the return of the best show on television."

"The Sopranos" won that label from virtually every critic last season. And for a show that is unarguably the most talked-about series ever on HBO, a channel that puts a premium on generating talk, the effort to reintroduce it to the public is extending just about everywhere HBO can reach. That includes HBO.com/Sopranos, of course, the most-used Web site ever associated with HBO, executives said. It features ersatz F.B.I. files on each character, gossip about who may be rubbed out and polls on the season's favorite lines of dialogue. (Last season's winner was uttered by Anthony Jr. in Episode 1, about the absence of his grandmother's cherished ziti. Like many "Sopranos" lines, it can't be printed here.)

Then there are the CD of songs from "The Sopranos," a music video, a traveling "waste management" truck (Tony's not-so-true calling), and a series of on-the-air promotions on multiple cable channels. There's even a promotion on a broadcast network, CBS, with the most prominent and expensive of those ads scheduled during the N.F.L. playoff games this weekend.

The promotional campaign is huge for HBO, both in significance and expenditure, though Mr. Kessler and other HBO executives declined to give an overall price. "Sopranos" images are so widespread, on display at bus stops as well as the entrance of Lincoln Tunnel, that some of the cast and crew are beginning to worry about a backlash. At the premiere party, James Gandolfini, who stars as Tony Soprano, said, sounding as if in character, "I'm sure people will be gunning for us this year."

Jeff Bewkes, HBO's chairman, said the pay cable channel was only trying to make up for "the big marketing disadvantage" it faced in comparison with the established broadcast networks. Only about 25 million subscribers receive HBO, about a quarter of the homes that are available to the broadcast networks.

"We are literally forced to buy buses," Mr. Bewkes said.

And trains. Mr. Kessler said HBO had also bought space on Metro North trains. That's just New York awareness, of course, he said. For more national exposure, HBO has turned to magazines like The New Yorker, Vanity Fair, People and Entertainment Weekly, all of which will be running a four-page ad on "The Sopranos."

Nothing is likely to be seen more widely than a commercial on an N.F.L. playoff game, but even there Mr. Bewkes said HBO was hamstrung. "CBS is the only network that will allow us to buy time," he said. And CBS forbids HBO to give the time and date of the "Sopranos" season premiere (Sunday at 9).

"Tony Soprano's Waste Management" truck will appear in parking lots at the N.F.L. playoff games and at the Super Bowl. Cardboard cutouts of the characters will be available for fans to pose with for pictures.

The channel also expects MTV or VH-1 to begin running a video featuring the show's theme song, "Woke Up This Morning," by the group A3.

This season's episodes include cameo appearances by people like Janeane Garofalo, Sandra Bernhard, Jon Favreau and Frank Sinatra Jr., all playing themselves.

Many of them joined to other celebrities at the premiere at the Ziegfield and the party at Roseland. It was one more indication of how far the show has come. Last year's premiere was in the basement of the Virgin Megastore on Broadway, and the party was at John's Pizzeria on West 44th Street.

—January 11, 2000

YOU CAN'T TELL THE PLAYERS WIDDOUT A SCORECARD

by J. Madison Davis

Former President,
The International Association of Crime Writers,
North America

it: his business as a "waste disposal consultant" is "trending downward." More deep rooted are moral crises. Tony is a guy who is moved to scary (to him), inexplicable tears when he remembers a family of migrating ducks that had made an extended stopover in his expensive swimming pool, then suddenly abandoned the pool to continue the flight north.

The seamlessness of the direction, the writing, the photography (here is

ted best actress in a drama for her rformance as Carmela Soprano, e Mafia boss's wife, a loving, word, common-sensical woman who pires to respectability.

The production was budgeted to ne in at $1.9 million to $2 million r episode, which would have made e total cost in the neighborhood of 5 million. That is small change by ndards in Hollywood, where $26 llion is not an outrageous budget a comparatively plain, contempoy two-hour movie. By th ndards, "The Soprano arly 13-hour feature fil ve cost $169 million, wit ring to sink the "Titanic In describing the prod he Sopranos," Mr. Chase und like the process by atoon of great comedy ed by Sid Caesar, put to minal Caesar shows of t cording to Mr. Chase, t

ase shared an award for the fifth episode. Edie ted best actress in a dra rformance as Carmela e Mafia boss's wife, a lo ed, common-sensical wo pires to respectability.

The production was bu ne in at $1.9 million to r episode, which would h e total cost in the neighb 5 million. That is small ndards in Hollywood, llion is not an outrageo a comparatively plain, y two-hour movie. By th ndards, "The Soprano arly 13-hour feature fil ve cost $169 million, wit ring to sink the "Titanic In describing the prod he Sopranos," Mr. Chase und like the process by atoon of great comedy ed by Sid Caesar, put to minal Caesar shows of t cording to Mr. Chase, t each "Sopranos" segm eet to discuss ideas, sometimes gmented by suggestions from er writers. Everybody chimed in. ch segment was shot fast — eight ys — though they often went into ertime. There was a good deal of shooting and a certain number of agreements. That is, everything s perfectly normal.

Mr. Chase's background is in telesion, commercial and cable, where credits as a producer, writer and ector include "The Rockford es," "I'll Fly Away" and "Northn Exposure." Nothing he had done fore, though, was preparation for e achievement of "The Sopranos." re is the comic, frequently torred journey toward self-awareness Tony Soprano, affluent suburban

psychiatrist, whose treatment of her patient résults in problems for both that Freud never dreamed of), Dominic Chianese (Tony's aging uncle and immediate mob superior, who is nearly undone by his longtime mistress) and Michael Imperioli (Tony's raging nephew, who aspires to be both a "made" man of the mob and a screenwriter). Dominating every scene she is in is Nancy Marchand as Tony's mother, a tough, emotionally stingy woman who wears a frown as her umbrella. It is she who instigates the kind of revenge on a son (he doesn't love her enough) to which only a mob widow and mother has access.

I saw "The Sopranos" not as it was initially broadcast

two. This gives the critic an e over the general public. Moment builds. Small but important det that might otherwise be forgot from one week to the next, or sim overlooked while one is attending the plot, remain vivid.

Yet such privileged viewing a has the potential to create the sor intimacy that makes it easier to s lapses' in continuity, contradicti within characters and a too-rea reliance on story formulas. "The nly survives such cl t also benefits from "Law and Order" d es are one way to est mate contact, syndi r.
I had never seen "L n first-run network te not long ago, I cau s a syndicated ser 11 P.M. five nights

hed four together, ree, but always at le ves the critic an e ral public. Moment but important deta otherwise be forgot k to the next, or sim hile one is attending ain vivid.

rivileged viewing a tial to create the sor makes it easier to s ntinuity, contradicti cters and a too-rea ory formulas. "The nly survives such cl t also benefits from "Law and Order" d es are one way to est mate contact, syndi r.
I had never seen "L n first-run network te not long ago, I cau s a syndicated ser 11 P.M. five nights

mpressions were goo excellent cast, decent writing, gr New York locations. "Law and der" seemed to be the sort of sh touted by friends who like to s things up when they call such tele sion dramas "the literature of time." Very quickly, however, I like talking back to the screen. Vie ings on successive nights did da age. Repeated plot ploys were quickly identified. Characters di become more complex with ti only more familiar, even when actors playing them were repla and the new characters were giv different names.

At best, "Law and Order" is soo ing. You know that, whether the c is won or lost, the same detecti

James Gandolfini *plays*

Anthony Soprano

It might seem strange to say that New Jersey crime boss Anthony (Tony) Soprano can't find the American dream, but that's what's wrong with him. Why can't his life be as idyllic as that of the ducks that stopped at his swimming pool and raised happy ducklings? Here he is at middle age. The proceeds from the family business are contracting. He gets no respect from his mother, Livia, or his uncle, Junior. His wife, Carmela, thinks he's spiritually empty, and his children, Meadow and Anthony Jr., show him as much deference as they would a presidential campaign commercial. He's tired of trying to solve everyone else's problems, but can't escape his sense of obligation to do so. Livia seems to be losing her mind, but no matter what he does for her; she, like Junior, compares him unfavorably with her sanitized memories of her late husband, "Johnny Boy."

Meantime, as in any business, there are lean and hungry young men who think an "old man" like Tony is limiting their possibilities. All this isn't what he aspired to. The value system he learned is disintegrating in ways he cannot understand. He can't control things like he thinks he should, and maybe it's because he's not up to being the leader he expected himself to be; for example, his solution to preventing a hit in his friend's restaurant is to order his men to burn the place down, rather than assert himself against his uncle.

At the same time, he can explode brutally, garroting a squealer while touring idyllic Maine colleges with his daughter, or ventilating one of Junior's henchmen. He's no Vito Corleone and can't grasp why. He wants it to be 1954 in his house, but it isn't. A guy like him shouldn't be taking Prozac and talking to a psychiatrist, but what's his choice?

JAMES GANDOLFINI earned a 1999 Emmy nomination and Television Critics Association award for his portrayal of Tony Soprano. A versatile actor, he has appeared in nearly two dozen movies and many episodes of various television series, but was astonished that he was chosen for the lead role.

"Look at this face," Gandolfini said to other cast members. "They took this face. What were they thinking?"

Everyone seemed to recognize his talent but him, and he has never had a better opportunity to show the extent of it. His more notable movies include *Fallen, A Civil Action, Twelve Angry Men* (on HBO), *Night Falls on Manhattan, She's So Lovely, The Juror, Get Shorty, Crimson Tide, and True Romance.* He was attracted to *The Sopranos* by the "bizarre" good writing in the scripts, in which sudden turns from humor to violence keep viewers off guard. Gandolfini very much appreciates the realism of the series-it is filmed in New Jersey, for one thing, where he was born in 1961. HBO also allows the program to approach subjects most television series avoid, and producer David Chase a creativity that would often be squelched.

Tony, says Gandolfini, "tries to do the right thing in his mind," but Tony's mind is nothing like the usual pseudo-Don's or series hero's. That's what makes his performance so realistic and powerful.

ted best actress in a drama for her
rformance as Carmela Soprano,
e Mafia boss's wife, a loving, wor-
d, common-sensical woman who
pires to respectability.

The production was budgeted to
me in at $1.9 million to $2 million
r episode, which would have made
e total cost in the neighborhood of
5 million. That is small change by
ndards in Hollywood, where $26
llion is not an outrageous budget
a comparatively plain, contempo-
ry two-hour movie. By th
ndards, "The Soprano
arly 13-hour feature fil
ve cost $169 million, wit
ing to sink the "Titanic
n describing the prod
he Sopranos," Mr. Chase
nd like the process by
atoon of great comedy
ed by Sid Caesar, put to
ninal Caesar shows of
cording to Mr. Chase, t

ase shared an award for
the fifth episode. Edie
ed best actress in a dra
formance as Carmela
Mafia boss's wife, a lo
d, common-sensical wo
pires to respectability.

he production was bu
ne in at $1.9 million to
episode, which would h
total cost in the neighb
million. That is small
ndards in Hollywood,
lion is not an outrageo
a comparatively plain,
y two-hour movie. By th
ndards, "The Soprano
arly 13-hour feature fil
ve cost $169 million, wit
ing to sink the "Titanic
n describing the prod
he Sopranos," Mr. Chase
nd like the process by
atoon of great comedy
ed by Sid Caesar, put to
ninal Caesar shows of
cording to Mr. Chase, t

each "Sopranos" segm
et to discuss ideas, sometimes
gmented by suggestions from the
er writers. Everybody chimed in.
ch segment was shot fast — eight
s — though they often went into
ertime. There was a good deal of
hooting and a certain number of
agreements. That is, everything
s perfectly normal.

Mr. Chase's background is in tele-
on, commercial and cable, where
credits as a producer, writer and
ctor include "The Rockford
es," "I'll Fly Away" and "North-
Exposure." Nothing he had done
ore, though, was preparation for
achievement of "The Sopranos."
re is the comic, frequently tor-
ed journey toward self-awareness
Tony Soprano affluent suburban

it: his business as a "waste disposal
consultant" is "trending downward." More deep rooted are moral
crises. Tony is a guy who is moved to
scary (to him), inexplicable tears
when he remembers a family of migrating ducks that had made an extended stopover in his expensive
swimming pool, then suddenly abandoned the pool to continue the flight
north.

The seamlessness of the direction,
the writing, the photography (here is

psychiatrist, whose treatment of her
patient results in problems for both
that Freud never dreamed of), Dominic Chianese (Tony's aging uncle
and immediate mob superior, who is
nearly undone by his longtime mistress) and Michael Imperioli (Tony's
raging nephew, who aspires to be
both a "made" man of the mob and a
screenwriter). Dominating every
scene she is in is Nancy Marchand as
Tony's mother, a tough, emotionally
stingy woman who wears a frown as
her umbrella. It is she who instigates
the kind of revenge on a son (he
doesn't love her enough) to which
only a mob widow and mother has
access.

I saw "The Sopranos" not as it was
initially broad

two. This gives the critic an e
over the general public. Moment
builds. Small but important det
that might otherwise be forgot
from one week to the next, or sim
overlooked while one is attending
the plot, remain vivid.

Yet such privileged viewing a
has the potential to create the sor
intimacy that makes it easier to s
lapses' in continuity, contradicti
within characters and a too-rea
reliance on story formulas. "The
nly survives such cl
t also benefits from
"Law and Order" d
es are one way to est
mate contact, syndi
r.
I had never seen "L
n first-run network t
not long ago, I cau
s a syndicated ser
11 P.M. five nights

hed four together,
ree, but always at le
ves the critic an ec
eral public. Moment
but important det
otherwise be forgot
k to the next, or sim
hile one is attending
ain vivid.
rivileged viewing a
tial to create the sort
makes it easier to s
ntinuity, contradicti
cters and a too-rea
ory formulas. "The
nly survives such cl
t also benefits from
"Law and Order" d
es are one way to est
mate contact, syndi
r.
I had never seen "L
n first-run network t
not long ago, I caug
s a syndicated ser
11 P.M. five nights

mpressions were goo
excellent cast, decent writing, gri
New York locations. "Law and
der" seemed to be the sort of sh
touted by friends who like to s
things up when they call such tele
sion dramas "the literature of
time." Very quickly, however, I
like talking back to the screen. Vie
ings on successive nights did da
age. Repeated plot ploys were
quickly identified. Characters did
become more complex with ti
only more familiar, even when
actors playing them were replac
and the new characters were giv
different names.

At best, "Law and Order" is soo
ing. You know that, whether the c
is won or lost, the same detecti

Edie Falco *plays*

Carmela Soprano

Carmela Soprano is, in some ways, tougher than Tony. While he can murder a man with his bare hands, she puts up with Tony's constant philandering and his depressions-not to mention her children's crises—and still has the energy to deal with Tony's mother. Maybe after eighteen years of marriage, she's developed the ability to not think too much about the machine guns and wads of cash in their heat ducts.

Carmela's only partly passive, however. She copes by buying furniture, secretly investing in the stock market, and trying to widen the social circles in which she and her husband move. There's Father Phil for spiritual solace, too-at least until she realizes that the priest uses food and DVDs to dance a little too close to the carnal flame of the lonely women he counsels. She's not afraid to confront Tony, wants to know everything that's going on, and doesn't hide her feelings.

An accomplished stage actress, **EDIE FALCO** says she researched the role of Carmela by being born into a boisterous Italian family, and by reverting to the Long Island accent that took four years of acting school to get rid of. She has appeared in over a dozen films, including *Trust, Bullets Over Broadway, The Funeral, Private Parts*, and *Copland*. She has also guested on television shows such as *Law and Order, Homicide: Life on the Streets, New York Undercover*, and HBO's Oz, and is the first Sopranos cast member to win an Emmy Award for her performance.

ted best actress in a drama for her
rformance as Carmela Soprano,
e Mafia boss's wife, a loving, wor-
d, common-sensical woman who
pires to respectability.

The production was budgeted to
me in at $1.9 million to $2 million
r episode, which would have made
e total cost in the neighborhood of
5 million. That is small change by
andards in Hollywood, where $26
llion is not an outrageous budget
a comparatively plain, contempo-
ry two-hour movie. By th
andards, "The Soprano
arly 13-hour feature fil
ve cost $169 million, wit
ying to sink the "Titanic.
In describing the prod
he Sopranos," Mr. Chase
und like the process by
atoon of great comedy
led by Sid Caesar, put to
minal Caesar shows of
ccording to Mr. Chase, t

ase shared an award for
the fifth episode. Edie
ted best actress in a dra
rformance as Carmela
e Mafia boss's wife, a lo
d, common-sensical wo
pires to respectability.

The production was bu
me in at $1.9 million to
r episode, which would h
e total cost in the neighb
5 million. That is small c
andards in Hollywood, v
llion is not an outrageo
a comparatively plain, c
ry two-hour movie. By th
andards, "The Soprano
arly 13-hour feature fil
ve cost $169 million, wit
ying to sink the "Titanic.
In describing the prod
he Sopranos," Mr. Chase
und like the process by
atoon of great comedy
led by Sid Caesar, put to
minal Caesar shows of
ccording to Mr. Chase, t

each "Sopranos" segme
eet to discuss ideas, sometimes
gmented by suggestions from the
er writers. Everybody chimed in.
ch segment was shot fast — eight
ys — though they often went into
ertime. There was a good deal of
shooting and a certain number of
sagreements. That is, everything
s perfectly normal.

Mr. Chase's background is in tele-
sion, commercial and cable, where
credits as a producer, writer and
rector include "The Rockford
es," "I'll Fly Away" and "North-
n Exposure." Nothing he had done
fore, though, was preparation for
e achievement of "The Sopranos."
re is the comic, frequently torred journey toward self-awareness

it: his business as a "waste disposal
consultant" is "trending downward." More deep rooted are moral
crises. Tony is a guy who is moved to
scary (to him), inexplicable tears
when he remembers a family of migrating ducks that had made an extended stopover in his expensive
swimming pool, then suddenly abandoned the pool to continue the flight
north.

The seamlessness of the direction,
the writing, the photography (here is

psychiatrist, whose treatment of her
patient results in problems for both
that Freud never dreamed of), Dominic Chianese (Tony's aging uncle
and immediate mob superior, who is
nearly undone by his longtime mistress) and Michael Imperioli (Tony's
raging nephew, who aspires to be
both a "made" man of the mob and a
screenwriter). Dominating every
scene she is in is Nancy Marchand as
Tony's mother, a tough, emotionally
stingy woman who wears a frown as
her umbrella. It is she who instigates
the kind of revenge on a son (he
doesn't love her enough) to which
only a mob widow and mother has
access.

I saw "The Sopranos" not as it was

two. This gives the critic an ed
over the general public. Momentu
builds. Small but important deta
that might otherwise be forgot
from one week to the next, or sim
overlooked while one is attending
the plot, remain vivid.

Yet such privileged viewing a
has the potential to create the sor
intimacy that makes it easier to s
lapses' in continuity, contradictio
within characters and a too-rea
reliance on story formulas. "The
nly survives such cl
t also benefits from
"Law and Order" d
es are one way to est
mate contact, syndi
r.
I had never seen "L
n first-run network te
not long ago, I caug
s a syndicated ser
11 P.M. five nights

hed four together,
ree, but always at le
ves the critic an ed
eral public. Momentu
but important deta
otherwise be forgot
k to the next, or sim
while one is attending
ain vivid.
rivileged viewing a
tial to create the sor
makes it easier to s
ntinuity, contradictio
cters and a too-rea
ory formulas. "The
nly survives such cl
t also benefits from
"Law and Order" d
es are one way to est
mate contact, syndi
r.
I had never seen "L
n first-run network te
not long ago, I caug
s a syndicated ser
11 P.M. five nights

mpressions were goo
excellent cast, decent writing, gri
New York locations. "Law and
der" seemed to be the sort of sh
touted by friends who like to s
things up when they call such tele
sion dramas "the literature of
time." Very quickly, however, I
like talking back to the screen. Vie
ings on successive nights did da
age. Repeated plot ploys were
quickly identified. Characters did
become more complex with ti
only more familiar, even when
actors playing them were repla
and the new characters were giv
different names.

At best, "Law and Order" is soo
ing. You know that, whether the c
is won or lost, the same detecti

Nancy Marchand *plays*

Livia Soprano

Producer and writer David Chase named Tony's mother, Livia, after a maternal aunt. However, she also shares the name of Augustus Caesar's ruthless, scheming wife in the celebrated BBC production of *I, Claudius*, which seems more than coincidental. In the first few episodes, she seems to be little more than a declining old woman-afraid to leave her house, afraid of being sent to a nursing home, constantly harping on the way things used to be. She soon, however, shows the manipulative and calculating character that leads to Dr. Melfi's opinion that she has a borderline personality disorder.

Tony is more direct in his diagnosis: He says his sisters fled her at the first opportunity, and that she wore his father down to a nub. She's been grinding on Tony as well. Nothing he or Carmela or anyone can do is adequate, whether it's buying the right pastry or cooking pork. Livia is too crafty to be direct, except with rude and meaningless complaints.

Once settled in the retirement home, Livia receives regular visits from Junior, and drops snippets of information that nudge him to various actions that he thinks come from his own muddled thinking. In short, she plays him like a fiddle. Only Tony seems to see through her facade of being addlepated, and remembers the way she crushed his father's plan of making a new start in Reno, Nevada. Nonetheless, these memories don't relieve Tony's guilt at dealing with her.

Carmela sees her for the monster she is, but treats her with respect for Tony's sake. At one point in the first season, Carmela mentions Junior's visits, which causes Livia to protest too much, as if she feels something for Junior that she shouldn't.

Livia is a bitter onion, layer upon layer of veiled possibilities. Is she willfully consenting to her son's murder, planting the idea in Junior's mind, or is it senility? Is she pretending to have memory lapses, or are they merely convenient? Is she faking her stroke, or is it a coincidence?

LIVIA is the second series television character that actor Nancy Marchand has brought vividly to life. Her role as Mrs. Pynchon in *Lou Grant* earned her four Emmys from 1978 to 1982, but she has appeared on numerous programs, going back to the *Philco Televison Playhouse* production of *Marty* in 1953; since then, she has guested on *Naked City, Beacon Hill, The Adams Chronicles, Cheers, Night Court*, and many others. She has been less active in film, appearing in *Tell Me That You Love Me, Junie Moon, The Hospital, Regarding Henry*, and *Jefferson in Paris*, among others.

Born in Buffalo, New York, in 1928, Marchand has had some health problems, and Livia was originally supposed to die at the end of the first season. Marchand made such a hit of the character, however, that Livia was given a reprieve to continue her evil ways into the second season.

ed best actress in a drama for her rformance as Carmela Soprano, Mafia boss's wife, a loving, word, common-sensical woman who pires to respectability.

The production was budgeted to me in at $1.9 million to $2 million r episode, which would have made total cost in the neighborhood of million. That is small change by ndards in Hollywood, where $26 llion is not an outrageous budget a comparatively plain, contempo-y two-hour movie. By th ndards, "The Soprano arly 13-hour feature fi ve cost $169 million, wit ing to sink the "Titanic n describing the prod he Sopranos," Mr. Chase nd like the process by atoon of great comedy ed by Sid Caesar, put to minal Caesar shows of cording to Mr. Chase, th

ase shared an award for the fifth episode. Edie F ted best actress in a dra rformance as Carmela Mafia boss's wife, a lo d, common-sensical wo pires to respectability.

The production was bu me in at $1.9 million to episode, which would h total cost in the neighb million. That is small ndards in Hollywood, v llion is not an outrageo a comparatively plain, y two-hour movie. By th ndards, "The Soprano arly 13-hour feature fi ve cost $169 million, wit ing to sink the "Titanic In describing the prod he Sopranos," Mr. Chase nd like the process by atoon of great comedy ed by Sid Caesar, put to minal Caesar shows of cording to Mr. Chase, th each "Sopranos" segm eet to discuss ideas, sometimes gmented by suggestions from the er writers. Everybody chimed in. ch segment was shot fast — eight ys — though they often went into ertime. There was a good deal of shooting and a certain number of sagreements. That is, everything s perfectly normal.

Mr. Chase's background is in tele-sion, commercial and cable, where credits as a producer, writer and ector include "The Rockford les," "I'll Fly Away" and "North-n Exposure." Nothing he had done fore, though, was preparation for achievement of "The Sopranos." re is the comic, frequently tor-ed journey toward self-awareness

it: his business as a "waste disposal consultant" is "trending down-ward." More deep rooted are moral crises. Tony is a guy who is moved to scary (to him), inexplicable tears when he remembers a family of mi-grating ducks that had made an ex-tended stopover in his expensive swimming pool, then suddenly aban-doned the pool to continue the flight north.

The seamlessness of the direction, the writing, the photography (here is

psychiatrist, whose treatment of her patient results in problems for both that Freud never dreamed of), Dom-inic Chianese (Tony's aging uncle and immediate mob superior, who is nearly undone by his longtime mis-tress) and Michael Imperioli (Tony's raging nephew, who aspires to be both a "made" man of the mob and a screenwriter). Dominating every scene she is in is Nancy Marchand as Tony's mother, a tough, emotionally stingy woman who wears a frown as her umbrella. It is she who instigates the kind of revenge on a son (he doesn't love her enough) to which only a mob widow and mother has access.

I saw "The Sopranos" not as it was

other time three, but always at le two. This gives the critic an ed over the general public. Moment builds. Small but important deta that might otherwise be forgot from one week to the next, or sim overlooked while one is attending the plot, remain vivid.

Yet such privileged viewing a has the potential to create the sor intimacy that makes it easier to s lapses' in continuity, contradictio within characters and a too-rea reliance on story formulas. "The nly survives such cl t also benefits from "Law and Order" d es are one way to est mate contact, syndi r.

I had never seen "L n first-run network te not long ago, I cau s a syndicated ser 11 P.M. five nights

hed four together, ree, but always at le ves the critic an ed ral public. Moment but important deta otherwise be forgot k to the next, or sim hile one is attending ain vivid.

rivileged viewing a tial to create the sor makes it easier to s tinuity, contradictio cters and a too-rea ory formulas. "The nly survives such cl t also benefits from "Law and Order" d es are one way to est mate contact, syndi r.

I had never seen "L n first-run network te not long ago, I cau s a syndicated ser 11 P.M. five nights

mpressions were goo excellent cast, decent writing, gr New York locations. "Law and der" seemed to be the sort of sh touted by friends who like to s things up when they call such tele sion dramas "the literature of time." Very quickly, however, I like talking back to the screen. Vi ings on successive nights did da age. Repeated plot ploys were quickly identified. Characters did become more complex with ti only more familiar, even when actors playing them were repla and the new characters were gi different names.

At best, "Law and Order" is soc ing. You know that, whether the is won or lost, the same detecti

Jamie Lynn Sigler *plays*

Meadow Soprano

Meadow Soprano, Tony's daughter, is sixteen-that horrible age when you never know whether you're going to be judged as a "young lady" or as a kid. Adults let you get a peek at their lives, then slam the door in your face.

Meadow is an honors student at Verbum Dei high school who plays volleyball and soccer. Tony beams with pride as she solos beautifully with the school choir. She wants to go to Berkeley—as far away from New Jersey as possible—but her parents suggest Colby, Bowdoin, or some place closer. Like all teenagers, she pushes her worldliness to assert her independence and adulthood—making out with a Dominican boy, or trying to talk about sex (and being silenced by Tony).

She's also not as sophisticated as she thinks.

Meadow knows her father is a member of the Mafia, yet isn't quite sure what that means, or how to react to it.

Playing Meadow is **JAMIE LYNN SIGLER**, who was nominated for the Young Star Award for "Best Performance in a TV Drama Series" for her work on *The Sopranos*. However, Sigler is already a veteran performer, having been enrolled in dance school by her parents at age three, and taking singing and acting lessons at age seven. She got her first professional role in a musical version of *It's a Wonderful Life*, and later appeared as the lead in *The Diary of Anne Frank*, and as Dorothy in *The Wiz*. Sigler has maintained an A average all through high school, and plans to major in psychology at New York University.

ted best actress in a drama for her performance as Carmela Soprano, the Mafia boss's wife, a loving, worried, common-sensical woman who aspires to respectability.

The production was budgeted to come in at $1.9 million to $2 million per episode, which would have made the total cost in the neighborhood of $26 million. That is small change by standards in Hollywood, where $26 million is not an outrageous budget for a comparatively plain, contemporary two-hour movie. By those standards, "The Sopranos," nearly 13-hour feature film, have cost $169 million, with trying to sink the "Titanic." In describing the production "The Sopranos," Mr. Chase sound like the process by a platoon of great comedy led by Sid Caesar, put together nal Caesar shows of according to Mr. Chase, the ase shared an award for the fifth episode. Edie ted best actress in a drama performance as Carmela Mafia boss's wife, a lov d, common-sensical wo pires to respectability.

The production was bu me in at $1.9 million to r episode, which would h total cost in the neighb million. That is small ndards in Hollywood, llion is not an outrageo a comparatively plain, ry two-hour movie. By th ndards, "The Soprano arly 13-hour feature fil ve cost $169 million, wit ing to sink the "Titanic In describing the prod he Sopranos," Mr. Chase und like the process by atoon of great comedy ed by Sid Caesar, put to minal Caesar shows of cording to Mr. Chase, th each "Sopranos" segm et to discuss ideas, sometimes gmented by suggestions from the er writers. Everybody chimed in. ch segment was shot fast — eight ys — though they often went into ertime. There was a good deal of hooting and a certain number of agreements. That is, everything s perfectly normal.

Mr. Chase's background is in television, commercial and cable, where credits as a producer, writer and ector include "The Rockford es," "I'll Fly Away" and "North- Exposure." Nothing he had done ore, though, was preparation for achievement of "The Sopranos." re is the comic, frequently tored journey toward self-awareness Tony Soprano, affluent suburban

It: his business as a "waste disposal consultant" is "trending downward." More deep rooted are moral crises. Tony is a guy who is moved to scary (to him), inexplicable tears when he remembers a family of migrating ducks that had made an extended stopover in his expensive swimming pool, then suddenly abandoned the pool to continue the flight north.

The seamlessness of the direction, the writing, the photography (here is

psychiatrist, whose treatment of her patient results in problems for both that Freud never dreamed of), Dominic Chianese (Tony's aging uncle and immediate mob superior, who is nearly undone by his longtime mistress) and Michael Imperioli (Tony's raging nephew, who aspires to be both a "made" man of the mob and a screenwriter). Dominating every scene she is in is Nancy Marchand as Tony's mother, a tough, emotionally stingy woman who wears a frown as her umbrella. It is she who instigates the kind of revenge on a son (he doesn't love her enough) to which only a mob widow and mother has access.

I saw "The Sopranos" not as it was initially broadcast at the rate of one

two. This gives the critic an e over the general public. Momen builds. Small but important det that might otherwise be forgo from one week to the next, or sim overlooked while one is attending the plot, remain vivid.

Yet such privileged viewing has the potential to create the sor intimacy that makes it easier to s lapses' in continuity, contradicti within characters and a too-re reliance on story formulas. "The nly survives such cl t also benefits from "Law and Order" d es are one way to est mate contact, synd r.

I had never seen "L n first-run network t not long ago, I cau s a syndicated se 11 P.M. five night

hed four together, ree, but always at le ves the critic an e eral public. Moment but important det otherwise be forgot k to the next, or sim hile one is attending ain vivid.

rivileged viewing a ial to create the sor makes it easier to s ntinuity, contradicti cters and a too-rea ory formulas. "The nly survives such clo t also benefits from "Law and Order" d es are one way to est mate contact, syndi r.

I had never seen "L n first-run network te not long ago, I cau s a syndicated ser 11 P.M. five nights

mpressions were goo excellent cast, decent writing, gri New York locations. "Law and der" seemed to be the sort of sh touted by friends who like to s things up when they call such tele sion dramas "the literature of time." Very quickly, however, I f like talking back to the screen. Vie ings on successive nights did da age. Repeated plot ploys were quickly identified. Characters did become more complex with tir only more familiar, even when t actors playing them were replac and the new characters were giv different names.

At best, "Law and Order" is soo ing. You know that, whether the ca is won or lost, the same detectiv

Robert Iler *plays*

Anthony Soprano, Jr.

At first glance, Anthony Soprano, Jr. is just a Nintendo-playing couch potato with a flippant irreverence for everything and distaste for his older sister. He downloads porn, gets into occasional fights, and is suspected of having Attention Deficit Disorder by the school counselor because he fidgets in class—in other words, he is an ordinary thirteen-year-old of the 1990s. When the boy with whom he's arranged a schoolyard fight timidly backs out, however, he first confronts what it means to be part of a mob family. He suddenly notices the government agents photographing the funeral of mob boss "Uncle Jackie" Aprile. And when an attempt is made on his father's life, he gets his first sense of the burden of being a Soprano.

ANTHONY, JR. is played with total authenticity by Robert Iler, who was discovered at age six by a talent agent as he walked down a street in Manhattan. He has appeared in many commercials, on *Saturday Night Live*, and in the film *Lessons in the Tie Code*. He attends public school in Manhattan.

rformance as Carmela Soprano,
Mafia boss's wife, a loving, wor-
ed, common-sensical woman who
pires to respectability.

The production was budgeted to
me in at $1.9 million to $2 million
r episode, which would have made
e total cost in the neighborhood of
6 million. That is small change by
andards in Hollywood, where $26
llion is not an outrageous budget
 a comparatively plain, contempo-
ry two-hour movie. By th

andards, "The Soprano
arly 13-hour feature fil
ve cost $169 million, wit
ying to sink the "Titanic
In describing the prod
he Sopranos," Mr. Chase
und like the process by
atoon of great comedy
led by Sid Caesar, put to
minal Caesar shows of
ccording to Mr. Chase, th

ase shared an award for
the fifth episode. Edie
ted best actress in a dra
rformance as Carmela
 Mafia boss's wife, a lo
ed, common-sensical wo
pires to respectability.

The production was bu
ne in at $1.9 million to
r episode, which would h
 total cost in the neighb
5 million. That is small
ndards in Hollywood, w
llion is not an outrageo
 a comparatively plain,
ry two-hour movie. By th
ndards, "The Soprano
arly 13-hour feature fil
ve cost $169 million, wit
ying to sink the "Titanic
In describing the prod
he Sopranos," Mr. Chase
und like the process by
ed by Sid Caesar, put to
minal Caesar shows of
cording to Mr. Chase, th
each "Sopranos" segme
et to discuss ideas, sometimes
gmented by suggestions from the
er writers. Everybody chimed in.
ch segment was shot fast — eight
ys — though they often went into
ertime. There was a good deal of
hooting and a certain number of
agreements. That is, everything
s perfectly normal.

Mr. Chase's background is in tele-
ion, commercial and cable, where
 credits as a producer, writer and
ector include "The Rockford
es," "I'll Fly Away" and "North-
 Exposure." Nothing he had done
ore, though, was preparation for
 achievement of "The Sopranos."
re is the comic, frequently tor-
ed journey toward self-awareness
Tony Soprano, affluent suburban

business as a "waste disposal
consultant" is "trending downward." More deep rooted are moral
crises. Tony is a guy who is moved to
scary (to him), inexplicable tears
when he remembers a family of migrating ducks that had made an extended stopover in his expensive
swimming pool, then suddenly abandoned the pool to continue the flight
north.

The seamlessness of the direction,
the writing, the photography (here is

psychiatrist, whose treatment of her
patient results in problems for both
that Freud never dreamed of), Dominic Chianese (Tony's aging uncle
and immediate mob superior, who is
nearly undone by his longtime mistress) and Michael Imperioli (Tony's
raging nephew, who aspires to be
both a "made" man of the mob and a
screenwriter). Dominating every
scene she is in is Nancy Marchand as
Tony's mother, a tough, emotionally
stingy woman who wears a frown as
her umbrella. It is she who instigates
the kind of revenge on a son (he
doesn't love her enough) to which
only a mob widow and mother has
access.

I saw "The Sopranos" not as it was
initially broadcast at the rate of one

two. This gives the critic an e
over the general public. Momen
builds. Small but important det
that might otherwise be forgo
from one week to the next, or sim
overlooked while one is attending
the plot, remain vivid.

Yet such privileged viewing a
has the potential to create the sor
intimacy that makes it easier to
lapses' in continuity, contradicti
within characters and a too-re
reliance on story formulas. "The
nly survives such cl
t also benefits from
"Law and Order" d
es are one way to es
mate contact, synd
r.

I had never seen "L
 first-run network t
 not long ago, I cau
s a syndicated se
11 P.M. five night

hed four together,
ree, but always at le
ves the critic an e
eral public. Moment
 but important det
otherwise be forgot
k to the next, or sim
hile one is attending
ain vivid.

rivileged viewing a
ial to create the sor
 makes it easier to s
tinuity, contradicti
cters and a too-rea
ory formulas. "The
nly survives such cl
t also benefits from
"Law and Order" d
es are one way to est
mate contact, syndi
r.

I had never seen "L
 first-run network te
 not long ago, I cau
s a syndicated ser
11 P.M. five nights

mpressions were goo
excellent cast, decent writing, gr
New York locations. "Law and
der" seemed to be the sort of sh
touted by friends who like to s
things up when they call such tele
sion dramas "the literature of
time." Very quickly, however, I
like talking back to the screen. Vie
ings on successive nights did da
age. Repeated plot ploys were
quickly identified. Characters did
become more complex with tir
only more familiar, even when
actors playing them were replac
and the new characters were giv
different names.

At best, "Law and Order" is soo
ing. You know that, whether the ca
is won or lost, the same detecti
and lawyers will be back tomo

Dominic Chianese *plays*

Uncle Junior

Corrado Enrico "Junior" Soprano is Tony's uncle, the older brother of the late "Johnny Boy" Soprano. He played catch with Tony when he was a kid, and has racked up two convictions in the "business." Like Tony, he doesn't know what the world is coming to—the younger generation doesn't have values, and the old codes seem to be falling apart. He commiserates with Livia about the crumbling of his world, and together they idealize the past. Tony isn't capable of running the family, he thinks—imagine a real man seeing a shrink!

Also like Tony, however, Junior's fantasy of the way things ought to be blinds him to the obvious. It's too easy for Tony to set him up as head of the family and lightning rod for federal investigators. Trying to show his strength, he taxes Hesh Rabkin (though "Johnny Boy" never did), refuses to move the hit planned for Artie Bucco's restaurant (though it would destroy his business), watches Mikey Palmice kill Christopher Moltisano's friend Brendan, and sets up Tony for a hit. Yet, when Tony survives, he defiantly refuses to violate the *omerta* by feeding Tony to the cops.

It would also be considered a sign of weakness for it to be known that Junior satisfies his woman orally. Even though she is one of the few refuges in his life, when the word finally does gets out, he does a Cagney on her with (appropriately enough) a pie, dumps her, and fires her.

Junior is played by **DOMINIC CHIANESE**, who began his career in 1952 touring in Gilbert and Sullivan's *The Mikado and Patience*. He has been very active on the stage and in television, appearing in episodes of *Kojak*, *East Side, West Side*, *Dark Shadows*, and *Law and Order*, among others. He's done his share of mob films, with *The Godfather Part II*, *The Lost Capone*, and *Gotti*. Chianese can also be seen in the films *Dog Day Afternoon*,

All the President's Men, Fort Apache: The Bronx, Night Falls on Manhattan, and the 1999 remake of The Thomas Crown Affair.

ed best actress in a drama for her
-formance as Carmela Soprano,
Mafia boss's wife, a loving, wor-
d, common-sensical woman who
pires to respectability.

he production was budgeted to
ne in at $1.9 million to $2 million
episode, which would have made
total cost in the neighborhood of
million. That is small change by
ndards in Hollywood, where $26
lion is not an outrageous budget
a comparatively plain, contempo-
y two-hour movie. By th
ndards, "The Soprano
arly 13-hour feature fil
e cost $169 million, wit
ing to sink the "Titanic
n describing the prod
he Sopranos," Mr. Chase
nd like the process by
toon of great comedy
ed by Sid Caesar, put tog
ninal Caesar shows of
cording to Mr. Chase, th

ase shared an award for
the fifth episode. Edie
ed best actress in a dram
-formance as Carmela
Mafia boss's wife, a lo
d, common-sensical wo
pires to respectability.
he production was bu
ne in at $1.9 million to
episode, which would h
total cost in the neighb
million. That is small
ndards in Hollywood,
lion is not an outrageo
a comparatively plain,
y two-hour movie. By th
ndards, "The Soprano
arly 13-hour feature fil
e cost $169 million, wit
ing to sink the "Titanic
n describing the prod
he Sopranos," Mr. Chase
nd like the process by
toon of great comedy
ed by Sid Caesar, put tog
ninal Caesar shows of t
cording to Mr. Chase, th
each "Sopranos" segme
et to discuss ideas, sometimes
gmented by suggestions from the
er writers. Everybody chimed in.
ch segment was shot fast — eight
vs — though they often went into
ertime. There was a good deal of
hooting and a certain number of
agreements. That is, everything
s perfectly normal.

Mr. Chase's background is in tele-
ion, commercial and cable, where
credits as a producer, writer and
ector include "The Rockford
es," "I'll Fly Away" and "North-
Exposure." Nothing he had done
ore, though, was preparation for
achievement of "The Sopranos."
re is the comic, frequently tor-
ed journey toward self-awareness

it: his business as a "waste disposal
consultant" is "trending downward." More deep rooted are moral
crises. Tony is a guy who is moved to
scary (to him), inexplicable tears
when he remembers a family of migrating ducks that had made an extended stopover in his expensive
swimming pool, then suddenly abandoned the pool to continue the flight
north.

The seamlessness of the direction,
the writing, the photography (here is

psychiatrist, whose treatment of her
patient results in problems for both
that Freud never dreamed of), Dominic Chianese (Tony's aging uncle
and immediate mob superior, who is
nearly undone by his longtime mistress) and Michael Imperioli (Tony's
raging nephew, who aspires to be
both a "made" man of the mob and a
screenwriter). Dominating every
scene she is in is Nancy Marchand as
Tony's mother, a tough, emotionally
stingy woman who wears a frown as
her umbrella. It is she who instigates
the kind of revenge on a son (he
doesn't love her enough) to which
only a mob widow and mother has
access.

I saw "The Sopranos" not as it was

two. This gives the critic an ed
over the general public. Momentu
builds. Small but important deta
that might otherwise be forgott
from one week to the next, or simp
overlooked while one is attending
the plot, remain vivid.

Yet such privileged viewing a
has the potential to create the sort
intimacy that makes it easier to s
lapses' in continuity, contradictio
within characters and a too-rea
reliance on story formulas. "The S
nly survives such clo
t also benefits from
"Law and Order" do
es are one way to esta
mate contact, syndi
r.

I had never seen "L
n first-run network te
not long ago, I caug
s a syndicated ser
11 P.M. five nights

hed four together,
ree, but always at le
ves the critic an ec
eral public. Momentu
but important deta
otherwise be forgott
k to the next, or sim
hile one is attending
ain vivid.

rivileged viewing a
tial to create the sort
makes it easier to s
ntinuity, contradictio
cters and a too-rea
ory formulas. "The
nly survives such clo
t also benefits from
"Law and Order" do
es are one way to est
mate contact, syndi
r.

I had never seen "L
n first-run network te
not long ago, I caug
s a syndicated ser
11 P.M. five nights

mpressions were goo
excellent cast, decent writing, gri
New York locations. "Law and
der" seemed to be the sort of sh
touted by friends who like to s
things up when they call such tele
sion dramas "the literature of
time." Very quickly, however, I
like talking back to the screen. Vie
ings on successive nights did da
age. Repeated plot ploys were
quickly identified. Characters did
become more complex with tir
only more familiar, even when
actors playing them were replac
and the new characters were gi
different names.

At best, "Law and Order" is soo
ing. You know that, whether the c
is won or lost, the same detecti

Lorraine Bracco *plays*

Dr. Jennifer Melfi

Dr. Jennifer Melfi, Tony Soprano's psychiatrist, is a beautiful Italian-American who is never sexier than when she is wearing her most professional coolness. She understands Tony's problems—at least from a theoretical viewpoint—but his passion and brutality are far from her world. A graduate of Tufts University Medical School, she has what appears to be a highly successful practice, but Tony fascinates and terrifies her.

When Dr. Cusimano's wife mocks the tacky Murano sculptures in Carmela's house, Melfi, with ambiguity in her voice, says she likes Murano. Her ex-husband belongs to an anti-defamation league and decries the Italian stereotyping in the media, but her son, a college student, points out to his father that Joe Columbo founded the organization.

Melfi is careful to avoid knowing anything specific about Tony's business, but is curious enough to stand awkwardly on a toilet at Dr. Cusimano's house to sneak a peak at Tony's house and imagine God-knows-what when she hears grunting coming from it. And even with the constant threat of danger—from both Tony and the mob—she continues to treat him. Does she really think she can handle an enraged Tony with a pair of scissors? Is she feeling an erotic fascination with the low, just as Tony is fascinated with her sexy, upper-class refinement?

LORRAINE BRACCO was an interesting choice for the role of Dr. Melfi, both because of her beauty and because of her playing the wife of mobster Henry Hill so notably in *Goodfellas*. She assumed the producers of the show were going to offer her another mob wife role, but life can often take strange turns.

Bracco was once voted the "Ugliest Girl in the Sixth Grade," according to one report, yet she became a fashion super-star after moving to France in 1974. She has a daughter by Harvey Keitel, but is currently married to Edward James

Olmos. She can be seen in *Hackers, Getting Gotti, Even Cowgirls Get the Blues, Medicine Man, Radio Flyer,* and *Sea of Love,* among her many films.

ted best actress in a drama for her
rformance as Carmela Soprano,
e Mafia boss's wife, a loving, wor-
ed, common-sensical woman who
pires to respectability.

The production was budgeted to
me in at $1.9 million to $2 million
r episode, which would have made
e total cost in the neighborhood of
6 million. That is small change by
andards in Hollywood, where $26
illion is not an outrageous budget
r a comparatively plain, contempo-
ry two-hour movie. By th
andards, "The Soprano
arly 13-hour feature fil
ave cost $169 million, wit
ying to sink the "Titanic
In describing the prod
The Sopranos," Mr. Chase
ound like the process by
atoon of great comedy
led by Sid Caesar, put to
eminal Caesar shows of t
ccording to Mr. Chase, th

hase shared an award for
the fifth episode. Edie F
oted best actress in a dra
erformance as Carmela
e Mafia boss's wife, a lo
ed, common-sensical wo
spires to respectability.

The production was bu
ome in at $1.9 million to
er episode, which would h
e total cost in the neighb
26 million. That is small
tandards in Hollywood,
iillion is not an outrageo
r a comparatively plain,
ary two-hour movie. By th
tandards, "The Soprano
early 13-hour feature fil
ave cost $169 million, wit
rying to sink the "Titanic
In describing the prod
The Sopranos," Mr. Chase
ound like the process by
latoon of great comedy
led by Sid Caesar, put to
eminal Caesar shows of t
ccording to Mr. Chase, th
f each "Sopranos" segm
neet to discuss ideas, sometimes
ugmented by suggestions from the
ther writers. Everybody chimed in.
ach segment was shot fast — eight
ays — though they often went into
vertime. There was a good deal of
eshooting and a certain number of
isagreements. That is, everything
vas perfectly normal.

Mr. Chase's background is in television, commercial and cable, where
his credits as a producer, writer and
director include "The Rockford
Files," "I'll Fly Away" and "Northern Exposure." Nothing he had done
before, though, was preparation for
the achievement of "The Sopranos."
Here is the comic, frequently tortured journey toward self-awareness

it: his business as a "waste disposal
consultant" is "trending downward." More deep rooted are moral
crises. Tony is a guy who is moved to
scary (to him), inexplicable tears
when he remembers a family of migrating ducks that had made an extended stopover in his expensive
swimming pool, then suddenly abandoned the pool to continue the flight
north.

The seamlessness of the direction,
the writing, the photography (here is

psychiatrist, whose treatment of her
patient results in problems for both
that Freud never dreamed of), Dominic Chianese (Tony's aging uncle
and immediate mob superior, who is
nearly undone by his longtime mistress) and Michael Imperioli (Tony's
raging nephew, who aspires to be
both a "made" man of the mob and a
screenwriter). Dominating every
scene she is in is Nancy Marchand as
Tony's mother, a tough, emotionally
stingy woman who wears a frown as
her umbrella. It is she who instigates
the kind of revenge on a son (he
doesn't love her enough) to which
only a mob widow and mother has
access.

I saw "The Sopranos" not as it was

two. This gives the critic an e
over the general public. Moment
builds. Small but important det
that might otherwise be forgo
from one week to the next, or sim
overlooked while one is attendin
the plot, remain vivid.

Yet such privileged viewing a
has the potential to create the sor
intimacy that makes it easier to s
lapses' in continuity, contradicti
within characters and a too-re
reliance on story formulas. "The
nly survives such c
t also benefits fror
"Law and Order" c
es are one way to es
mate contact, synd
r.

I had never seen "
n first-run network
not long ago, I ca
s a syndicated se
11 P.M. five nigh

hed four together,
ree, but always at l
yes the critic an e
ral public. Momen
but important det
otherwise be forgo
k to the next, or sir
hile one is attendin
ain vivid.

rivileged viewing
tial to create the so
makes it easier to
ntinuity, contradict
cters and a too-re
ory formulas. "The
nly survives such c
t also benefits fror
"Law and Order"
es are one way to es
mate contact, sync
r.

I had never seen "
n first-run network
not long ago, I ca
s a syndicated se
11 P.M. five nigh

mpressions were g
excellent cast, decent writing, g
New York locations. "Law and
der" seemed to be the sort of s
touted by friends who like to
things up when they call such te
sion dramas "the literature of
time." Very quickly, however,
like talking back to the screen. V
ings on successive nights did c
age. Repeated plot ploys were
quickly identified. Characters d
become more complex with
only more familiar, even wher
actors playing them were repl
and the new characters were g
different names.

At best, "Law and Order" is s
ing. You know that, whether the
is won or lost, the same detec

Michael Imperioli *plays*

Christopher Moltisano

Christopher Moltisano is a soldier of the MTV generation. His literature is the motion picture, and his nightmare is a life without a plot curve. He wants success quick and he wants it easy, constantly grousing about not being a "made" man yet, despite whacking a Czech gangster and finishing off Mikey Almice. It's a material world for Chris, and he doesn't understand why he should be living in a cheap apartment, never mind his $60,000 Lexus. He's also happy to take a toot of cocaine now and again, which doesn't help him develop any patience—there *must* be a quicker way to the top, he thinks. He gets himself screenplay books and sets out to write a mob picture on a stolen laptop, which doesn't seem to come with a spell checker. In the second season, though, Chris manages to get involved with an independent film that features Janeane Garofalo and Sandra Bernhard as lesbian lovers.

When pressed, Moltisano shows more loyalty to those around him than one would expect. He decides to stay out of a heist his friend Brendan has planned against Tony's orders, but when it goes awry, he tries to get Brendan off the hook. He's devoted to his girlfriend Adrianna, a waitress with aspirations to be a music manager. He pays for the studio and arranges for her to make a contract with a record company, even though he comes to realize that the group stinks.

The failures of his fantasies always keep his anger simmering. Why *not* make racial insults in an African-American burger joint? Why not shoot a pastry shop clerk in the foot?

MICHAEL IMPERIOLI plays the role of Christopher, and has appeared in nearly forty movies since 1988, when he was only twenty-two. He was recently a producer and writer for the Spike Lee film *Summer of Sam*, and will be writing one of the episodes for the second season of The *Sopranos*, so we can assume that, unlike the character he plays, he knows how to spell. Among the more notable movies he has appeared in are *Trees Lounge*, *I Shot Andy Warhol*, *Dead Presidents*, *Malcolm X*, and *Lean on Me*. In *Goodfellas*, he plays "Spider," who is shot in the foot by Joe Pesci, and which is alluded to in Moltisano's shooting of the bakery clerk.

ted best actress in a drama for her
rformance as Carmela Soprano,
e Mafia boss's wife, a loving, wor-
d, common-sensical woman who
pires to respectability.

The production was budgeted to
me in at $1.9 million to $2 million
r episode, which would have made
e total cost in the neighborhood of
5 million. That is small change by
andards in Hollywood, where $26
llion is not an outrageous budget
· a comparatively plain, contempo-
ry two-hour movie. By th
andards, "The Soprano
arly 13-hour feature fil
ve cost $169 million, wit
ring to sink the "Titanic
In describing the prod
he Sopranos," Mr. Chase
und like the process by
atoon of great comedy
led by Sid Caesar, put to
minal Caesar shows of
ccording to Mr. Chase, t

ase shared an award for
the fifth episode. Edie F
ted best actress in a dram
rformance as Carmela
e Mafia boss's wife, a lo
d, common-sensical wo
pires to respectability.

The production was bu
me in at $1.9 million to
r episode, which would h
e total cost in the neighb
5 million. That is small c
andards in Hollywood, v
llion is not an outrageo
a comparatively plain, c
ry two-hour movie. By th
andards, "The Soprano
arly 13-hour feature fil
ve cost $169 million, wit
ring to sink the "Titanic
In describing the prod
he Sopranos," Mr. Chase
und like the process by
atoon of great comedy
led by Sid Caesar, put to
minal Caesar shows of t
ccording to Mr. Chase, th
each "Sopranos" segm
eet to discuss ideas, sometimes
gmented by suggestions from the
her writers. Everybody chimed in.
ach segment was shot fast — eight
ys — though they often went into
ertime. There was a good deal of
shooting and a certain number of
sagreements. That is, everything
as perfectly normal.

Mr. Chase's background is in tele-
sion, commercial and cable, where
s credits as a producer, writer and
rector include "The Rockford
les," "I'll Fly Away" and "North-
n Exposure." Nothing he had done
fore, though, was preparation for
e achievement of "The Sopranos."
ere is the comic, frequently torred journey toward self-awareness
Tony Soprano, affluent suburban

it: his business as a "waste disposal
consultant" is "trending downward." More deep rooted are moral
crises. Tony is a guy who is moved to
scary (to him), inexplicable tears
when he remembers a family of migrating ducks that had made an extended stopover in his expensive
swimming pool, then suddenly abandoned the pool to continue the flight
north.

The seamlessness of the direction,
the writing, the photography (here is

psychiatrist, whose treatment of her
patient results in problems for both
that Freud never dreamed of), Dominic Chianese (Tony's aging uncle
and immediate mob superior, who is
nearly undone by his longtime mistress) and Michael Imperioli (Tony's
raging nephew, who aspires to be
both a "made" man of the mob and a
screenwriter). Dominating every
scene she is in is Nancy Marchand as
Tony's mother, a tough, emotionally
stingy woman who wears a frown as
her umbrella. It is she who instigates
the kind of revenge on a son (he
doesn't love her enough) to which
only a mob widow and mother has
access.

I saw "The Sopranos" not as it was

two. This gives the critic an e
over the general public. Momen
builds. Small but important det
that might otherwise be forgo
from one week to the next, or sim
overlooked while one is attendin
the plot, remain vivid.

Yet such privileged viewing
has the potential to create the so
intimacy that makes it easier to s
lapses' in continuity, contradict
within characters and a too-re
reliance on story formulas. "The
nly survives such c
t also benefits fror
"Law and Order"
es are one way to es
mate contact, synd
r.

I had never seen "
h first-run network
not long ago, I ca
s a syndicated se
11 P.M. five nigh

hed four together,
ree, but always at l
ves the critic an e
eral public. Momen
but important det
otherwise be forgo
k to the next, or sim
hile one is attendin
ain vivid.

rivileged viewing
tial to create the so
makes it easier to s
ntinuity, contradict
cters and a too-re
ory formulas. "The
nly survives such c
t also benefits fror
"Law and Order"
es are one way to es
mate contact, synd
r.

I had never seen "I
h first-run network t
not long ago, I ca
s a syndicated se
11 P.M. five night

mpressions were go
excellent cast, decent writing, g
New York locations. "Law and
der" seemed to be the sort of s
touted by friends who like to
things up when they call such tel
sion dramas "the literature of
time." Very quickly, however, I
like talking back to the screen. V
ings on successive nights did d
age. Repeated plot ploys were
quickly identified. Characters di
become more complex with ti
only more familiar, even when
actors playing them were repla
and the new characters were g
different names.

At best, "Law and Order" is so
ing. You know that, whether the
is won or lost, the same detect

Vincent Pastore *plays*

Big Pussy

Pussy "Big Pussy" Bompensiero is one of Tony's inner circle, a reliable soldier. He disappeared in episode 11 of the first season, much to Tony's distress. Alcoholic detective Vin Makasian (played by John Heard) said that Pussy was wearing a wire for the Feds and Tony was ninety percent certain it was true. Pussy was a good man, and he and Tony went way back, but with three kids in college and the business slacking off, he might have cut a deal. Didn't his back pain and the Percodans, Tony wonders, indicate he was under great stress? Only at the last moment did Tony discover who was really wearing the wire, and that Vin owed Pussy thousands in gambling debts. But Pussy, meanwhile, mysteriously vanished. Witness protection? Sleeping with the fishes? Pussy returns in the second season, and answers will be given.

VINCENT (VINNY) PASTORE, who plays Pussy, owned a club in New Rochelle, New York, frequented by Matt and Kevin Dillon, who persuaded him to try acting. He's become a more and more familiar face through the 1990s, especially in such gangster films as *Goodfellas, Gotti, Who Do I Gotta Kill?, Witness to the Mob, and The Last Don.* He has also frequently appeared on the television series *Law and Order.*

ed best actress in a drama for her [per]formance as Carmela Soprano, [th]e Mafia boss's wife, a loving, wor[l]d, common-sensical woman who [as]pires to respectability.

The production was budgeted to [co]me in at $1.9 million to $2 million [per] episode, which would have made [th]e total cost in the neighborhood of [2]5 million. That is small change by [sta]ndards in Hollywood, where $26 [mi]llion is not an outrageous budget [for] a comparatively plain, contempo[ra]ry two-hour movie. By th[e] [sta]ndards, "The Soprano[s," a ne]arly 13-hour feature fil[m would ha]ve cost $169 million, wit[h noth]ing to sink the "Titanic[." In describing the proc[ess of] [T]he Sopranos," Mr. Chase [...] [so]und like the process by [which a pl]atoon of great comedy [writers] led by Sid Caesar, put to[gether the se]minal Caesar shows of t[he 1950's. Ac]cording to Mr. Chase, t[he writers]

[Mr. Ch]ase shared an award for [writing] the fifth episode. Edie F[alco...] [vo]ted best actress in a dra[ma for her] [pe]rformance as Carmela [Soprano,] [th]e Mafia boss's wife, a lo[ving, wor-] [l]d, common-sensical wo[man who] [as]pires to respectability.

The production was bu[dgeted to] [co]me in at $1.9 million to [$2 million] [pe]r episode, which would h[ave made] [th]e total cost in the neighb[orhood of] [2]5 million. That is small c[hange by] [sta]ndards in Hollywood, v[where $26] [mil]lion is not an outrageo[us budget] [for] a comparatively plain, c[ontempo-] [ra]y two-hour movie. By th[e] [sta]ndards, "The Soprano[s," a ne-] [ear]ly 13-hour feature fil[m would ha-] [ve] cost $169 million, wit[h nothing] In describing the proc[ess...] [T]he Sopranos," Mr. Chase [...] [so]und like the process by [which a pl-] led by Sid Caesar, put to[gether...] [mi]nal Caesar shows of t[he...] [ac]cording to Mr. Chase, t[he writers] each "Sopranos" segm[ent...] [m]eet to discuss ideas, sometimes [se]gmented by suggestions from the [ot]her writers. Everybody chimed in. [Ea]ch segment was shot fast — eight [da]ys — though they often went into [ov]ertime. There was a good deal of [re]shooting and a certain number of [di]sagreements. That is, everything [a]s perfectly normal.

Mr. Chase's background is in tele[vi]sion, commercial and cable, where [i]s credits as a producer, writer and [di]rector include "The Rockford [Fi]les," "I'll Fly Away" and "North[er]n Exposure." Nothing he had done [be]fore, though, was preparation for [th]e achievement of "The Sopranos." [He]re is the comic, frequently tor[tu]red journey toward self-awareness

it: his business as a "waste disposal consultant" is "trending downward." More deep rooted are moral crises. Tony is a guy who is moved to scary (to him), inexplicable tears when he remembers a family of migrating ducks that had made an extended stopover in his expensive swimming pool, then suddenly abandoned the pool to continue the flight north.

The seamlessness of the direction, the writing, the photography (here is

psychiatrist, whose treatment of her patient results in problems for both that Freud never dreamed of), Dominic Chianese (Tony's aging uncle and immediate mob superior, who is nearly undone by his longtime mistress) and Michael Imperioli (Tony's raging nephew, who aspires to be both a "made" man of the mob and a screenwriter). Dominating every scene she is in is Nancy Marchand as Tony's mother, a tough, emotionally stingy woman who wears a frown as her umbrella. It is she who instigates the kind of revenge on a son (he doesn't love her enough) to which only a mob widow and mother has access.

I saw "The Sopranos" not as it was

two. This gives the critic an e[dge] over the general public. Moment[um] builds. Small but important det[ail] that might otherwise be forgot[ten] from one week to the next, or sim[ply] overlooked while one is attending [to] the plot, remain vivid.

Yet such privileged viewing a[lso] has the potential to create the sor[t of] intimacy that makes it easier to s[ee] lapses' in continuity, contradicti[ons] within characters and a too-re[ady] reliance on story formulas. "The [...] [o]nly survives such cl[ose...] [bu]t also benefits fro[m...] "Law and Order" d[...] [es] are one way to est[ablish...] [inti]mate contact, synd[ication] [...]r.

I had never seen "L[aw...] [...] first-run network [...] [...] not long ago, I cau[ght] [...] a syndicated se[ries...] 11 P.M. five night[s...]

[...]hed four together, [th]ree, but always at le[ast] [gi]ves the critic an e[dge] [gen]eral public. Moment[um] [...] but important det[ails] [...] otherwise be forgo[tten] [...]k to the next, or sim[ply] [...]hile one is attending [...]ain vivid.

[...]privileged viewing a[lso] [...]tial to create the sor[t] [...] makes it easier to s[ee] [...]ntinuity, contradicti[ons] [...]cters and a too-re[ady] [...]ory formulas. "The [...] [o]nly survives such c[lose...] [...]t also benefits fro[m...] "Law and Order" [...] [...]es are one way to es[t...] [...]mate contact, synd[...] [...]r.

I had never seen "L[aw...] [...] first-run network [...] [...] not long ago, I cau[ght] [...] a syndicated se[ries...] 11 P.M. five night[s...]

[im]pressions were go[od...] excellent cast, decent writing, g[ood] New York locations. "Law [and Or-] [der]" seemed to be the sort of s[how] touted by friends who like to [jazz] things up when they call such tel[evi-] sion dramas "the literature of [our] time." Very quickly, however, I [felt] like talking back to the screen. V[iew-] ings on successive nights did d[...] age. Repeated plot ploys were [...] quickly identified. Characters d[id not] become more complex with [...] only more familiar, even when [the] actors playing them were repl[aced] and the new characters were g[iven] different names.

At best, "Law and Order" is s[ooth-] ing. You know that, whether the [case] is won or lost, the same detect[ives]

"Little" Steven Van Zandt *plays*

Silvio Dante

Silvio Dante is another member of Tony's inner circle who runs the Badda Bing! club. With his hair (is that a rug, or what?) a particularly unnatural color, Silvio looks a bit like *Saturday Night Live* comedian Kevin Nealon doing a skit. He is so obviously a mobster, and his comments about raising kids in the information age, or his arguments with a referee at his daughter's oh-so-suburban soccer game seem particularly otherworldly.

STEVEN VAN ZANDT, a guitarist with Bruce Springsteen's E Street Band, was considered for the role of Tony Soprano, even though he had never acted before. When asked to play another part, he was-n't sure he wanted to take a role away from a real actor, so Silvio was written in. Notice the inside joke that Silvio is said to have owned rock clubs in Asbury Park.

ed best actress in a drama for her
rformance as Carmela Soprano,
e Mafia boss's wife, a loving, wor-
d, common-sensical woman who
pires to respectability.

The production was budgeted to
me in at $1.9 million to $2 million
r episode, which would have made
e total cost in the neighborhood of
5 million. That is small change by
ndards in Hollywood, where $26
llion is not an outrageous budget
a comparatively plain, contempo-
y two-hour movie. By th
ndards, "The Soprano
arly 13-hour feature fi
ve cost $169 million, wit
ing to sink the "Titanic
In describing the proc
he Sopranos," Mr. Chase
nd like the process by
atoon of great comedy
led by Sid Caesar, put to
minal Caesar shows of t
cording to Mr. Chase, th

ase shared an award for
the fifth episode. Edie
ted best actress in a dra
rformance as Carmela
e Mafia boss's wife, a lo
d, common-sensical wo
pires to respectability.
The production was bu
me in at $1.9 million to
r episode, which would h
e total cost in the neighb
5 million. That is small c
ndards in Hollywood, v
llion is not an outrageo
a comparatively plain, c
y two-hour movie. By th
ndards, "The Soprano
arly 13-hour feature fil
ve cost $169 million, wit
ing to sink the "Titanic
In describing the prod
he Sopranos," Mr. Chase
nd like the process by
atoon of great comedy
led by Sid Caesar, put to
minal Caesar shows of t
cording to Mr. Chase, th
each "Sopranos" segm
eet to discuss ideas, sometimes
gmented by suggestions from the
er writers. Everybody chimed in.
ch segment was shot fast — eight
ys — though they often went into
ertime. There was a good deal of
shooting and a certain number of
sagreements. That is, everything
s perfectly normal.

Mr. Chase's background is in tele-
sion, commercial and cable, where
s credits as a producer, writer and
ector include "The Rockford
les," "I'll Fly Away" and "North-
n Exposure." Nothing he had done
fore, though, was preparation for
e achievement of "The Sopranos."
ere is the comic, frequently torred journey toward self-awareness

it: his business as a "waste disposal
consultant" is "trending downward." More deep rooted are moral
crises. Tony is a guy who is moved to
scary (to him), inexplicable tears
when he remembers a family of migrating ducks that had made an extended stopover in his expensive
swimming pool, then suddenly abandoned the pool to continue the flight
north.

The seamlessness of the direction,
the writing, the photography (here is

psychiatrist, whose treatment of her
patient results in problems for both
that Freud never dreamed of), Dominic Chianese (Tony's aging uncle
and immediate mob superior, who is
nearly undone by his longtime mistress) and Michael Imperioli (Tony's
raging nephew, who aspires to be
both a "made" man of the mob and a
screenwriter). Dominating every
scene she is in is Nancy Marchand as
Tony's mother, a tough, emotionally
stingy woman who wears a frown as
her umbrella. It is she who instigates
the kind of revenge on a son (he
doesn't love her enough) to which
only a mob widow and mother has
access.

I saw "The Sopranos" not as it was

other time three, but always at l
two. This gives the critic an e
over the general public. Moment
builds. Small but important det
that might otherwise be forgot
from one week to the next, or sim
overlooked while one is attending
the plot, remain vivid.

Yet such privileged viewing a
has the potential to create the sor
intimacy that makes it easier to s
lapses' in continuity, contradicti
within characters and a too-rea
reliance on story formulas. "The

nly survives such cl
t also benefits from
"Law and Order" d
es are one way to est
mate contact, syndi
r.

I had never seen "L
n first-run network t
not long ago, I cau
s a syndicated ser
11 P.M. five nights

hed four together,
ree, but always at le
ves the critic an e
eral public. Moment
but important det
otherwise be forgot
k to the next, or sim
hile one is attending
ain vivid.

rivileged viewing a
tial to create the sor
makes it easier to s
ntinuity, contradicti
cters and a too-rea
ory formulas. "The

nly survives such cl
t also benefits from
"Law and Order" d
es are one way to est
mate contact, syndi
r.

I had never seen "L
n first-run network t
not long ago, I cau
s a syndicated ser
11 P.M. five night

mpressions were go
excellent cast, decent writing, gr
New York locations. "Law and
der" seemed to be the sort of sh
touted by friends who like to
things up when they call such tel
sion dramas "the literature of
time." Very quickly, however, I
like talking back to the screen. V
ings on successive nights did d
age. Repeated plot ploys were
quickly identified. Characters di
become more complex with ti
only more familiar, even when
actors playing them were repla
and the new characters were g
different names.

At best, "Law and Order" is so
ing. You know that, whether the
is won or lost, the same detect

Tony Sirico *plays*

Paulie Walnuts

The third soldier Tony can always rely on is Paulie Walnuts, who got his name either from the hardness of his head or his mistake in hijacking a truckload of walnuts instead of televisions. He is a tattooed, old-fashioned thug with a few "issues" of his own-something about women, it seems. He even consulted a therapist, though he can't get his head around Tony going to a female psychiatrist. He's a movie buff, quick with a quip, but deadly as a cobra. And-Madonn'!- does he hate poison ivy!

Paulie is played with an interesting mixture of humor and utter cruelty by **TONY SIRICO**, who grew up poor and wanted to be like the gangsters he saw on the streets. Sometimes listed in the credits as Anthony Sirico or G. Anthony Sirico, he's been in many gangster movies, including *Godfather Part II*, *Miller's Crossing*, *Goodfellas*, and *Mickey Blue Eyes*, but he's also been a regular in Woody Allen films, appearing in *Deconstructing Harry*, *Celebrity*, *Everyone Says I Love You*, *Mighty Aphrodite*, and *Bullets Over Broadway*.

Jerry Adler *plays*

"Hesh" Rabkin

Herman "Hesh" Rabkin has always been one of the inner circle of the Soprano family and was always trusted by Johnny Boy as a consigliere. A Jew (do we hear the whisper of Meyer Lansky here?), Hesh can never be a made man, but that doesn't decrease his stature; gangsters weren't *all* Italians, after all. Hesh, however, has worked with his brain more than his muscle—he's a negotiator, not a fighter, but that doesn't mean he's weak. He was the front man for F-Note Records ("Johnny Boy" was the silent partner), which exploited black artists and looted their royalties. Now, he provides credit for those who can't get loans at Chase Manhattan, and finds peace in contemplating the horses on his farm.

JERRY ADLER plays Hesh, and has worked with producer/writer David Chase before on the quirky television hit *Northern Exposure*. He has worked on a number of other television series, including *Mad About You* and *Hudson Street*. He is familiar to viewers as the neighbor that Larry Lipton (Woody Allen) suspects of killing his wife in the film *Manhattan Murder Mystery*.

And The Sister

Aida Turturro *plays*

Janice Soprano

Janice Soprano is one of the sisters who ran away from Livia Soprano as soon as she was able, but because of Livia's stroke, she returns to New Jersey in the second season. Only mentioned in passing during the first season, Janice is described by Tony as a "fucking wanna be dot-head" who has taken the name "Vishnamatha or somethin'." She turns up in the second season to give Tony even more headaches as she schemes to nose her way into the business.

AIDA TURTURRO was persuaded by James Gandolfini to try for the role; they had previously worked together in a revival of *A Streetcar Named Desire*. Actors John and Nicholas Turturro are her cousins. She has appeared in dozens of films, including *Bringing Out the Dead, Mickey Blue Eyes, Fallen, Sleepers, Manhattan Murder Mystery, Tales of Erotica*, and *What About Bob?* She also been active on stage, and did a stint as Fran on the daytime soap opera *As the World Turns*.

AFTERWORD

ABOUT DAVID CHASE

by Stephen J. Cannell

In the mid-seventies, I was the Writer/Producer and Co-creator of *The Rockford Files*. Our close knit staff consisted of Juanita Bartlett, Charles Johnson, and our Executive Producer, Meta Rosenberg.

Juanita and I had just completed a grueling season, where the two of us had written seventeen of the twenty-two episodes. We told Meta that we didn't think we could pull off another year like that. Meta, who was always on the prowl for new writers, told us that she had found a wonderful new talent and quickly passed around a few scripts by a little-known writer named David Chase. I read his material and, not wanting to admit too much—ego being what it is in Hollywood—I reluctantly agreed that he "showed some promise." Quickly, Juanita and I accepted David onto our writing staff.

David arrived a few mornings later and was assigned an office across the hall from mine. I remember him as slender, with a shy demeanor, offset by mischievous eyes and a dark, rapier-quick wit.

There was little chance to really get acquainted that morning, as Juanita and I were locked up, banging out scripts for the upcoming season; but that afternoon, we broke off some time to plot a story for David. It was our practice on *Rockford* to work stories in a group, but only one of us would write the actual script.

At that time, I was riding very high at the studio, having created *The Rockford Files*, as well as *Baretta* and *Black Sheep Squadron*. I thought I had the best fastball on the lot. Of course, Steve Bochco was just two buildings away, smokin' 'em over the plate. But hey, I was in my early thirties and still invested in my ego fantasies.

A week or ten days later, David turned in his first draft. So, now I have sixty pages from the "new kid," David Chase, or DeCesare; as I had come to learn, that was his off-the-boat family name.

I picked up David's work fearing the worst. After all, how could anybody but Juanita and I really capture the essence of our show, which we viewed as a tone poem for the seventies? I was fully expecting a bag of dirt as I cracked open the script.

An hour later, I had a huge dilemma.

My problem?

I thought David's script was funnier and better written than any screenplay I had done for the show in the last two seasons. How could this be happening? And worse still, how do I face this creative competition from twenty feet across the hall? Do I criticize his work? Hector this DeCesare guy, attack his confidence with the hope I might take a little spin off his curve? Or, do I go down the hall, throw my arms around him and tell him how great the damn thing really is?

Fortunately for the show, I elected the latter.

For the next three years, David became a critical part of our Writing/Producing team, providing us with some of the funniest moments and best scripts on that series.

Your writing colleagues on a show are like family. On *Rockford*, we had a matriarchal society, with Meta as our headmistress and David, Charles, Juanita and I as the siblings. David was the younger brother who could always find the twists on a theme and mine dark humor that went well beyond what I saw elsewhere on television.

The way his mind worked fascinated me. David always saw things from a unique and totally original point of view.

Two quick stories and one observation:

We were sitting around one day during the third *Rockford* season, trying to come up with a story for Juanita to write. She had been, as luck (or sexism) would have it, stuck writing about hookers for her last couple of shows. She entered my office saying, "I'll write anything except another story about a damned hooker." David and I smiled and nodded impishly and then, just to give her a little grief, I said, "I've got an idea. Listen to this: A murder; but the only clue is a soapy washcloth with the logo, 'Pimp Daddy Motel' on the corner, and then . . ."

"No hookers," she said, grinning; but she was serious. She wasn't going near another one.

All this time, David remained silent on the couch, off somewhere else (I thought). Juanita and I started hunting around for something for her to really write, when suddenly, David piped up, "Let's do it."

"Do what?" Juanita and I asked.

"A hooker. But, here's the catch," he grinned. "She'll be a hooker with a heart of gold."

"*David,*" Juanita said, laughing. "That's the oldest cliché in film . . . and I'm not kidding. I'm not doing another story about a prostitute."

"But, what if this girl is a tragic creature," David pushed on. "She has this huge crush on Rockford, but Rockford doesn't see it . . . doesn't know she's in love with him. He sees her only as a friend. She's this very sweet person who's always helping everyone. She's going to beauty school, trying to better herself, to make her life into something, all the time asking Rockford for dumb beauty parlor career advice, hoping he'll fall for her and . . ."

. . . Rita Kapcovitch was born.

Some time after lunch, we had the story. Juanita wrote the script (beautifully) and it won an Emmy for Rita Moreno, who played the part. But for me, this was typical David Chase. I was kidding; Juanita was adamant; but it was David, who saw a way to take the oldest cliché in film and put a dark, funny twist on it so Juanita could serve it up fresh with mustard.

Many years later—in fact, just a few years ago—we were doing *The Rockford Files* reunion movies and again, I was treated to my friend David's twisty mind; which, I have come to suspect, is the only one remotely like it on the planet!

We had plotted a two-hour story for me to write. It was about a mob boss named Joseph Cortello, whose street moniker was, for some reason unknown to Rockford, "Happy."

"I don't think they call him 'Happy' because he smiles a lot," Rockford mused darkly, on page ten of my script.

We come to learn that he got that name because he is manic-depressive and would giggle from adrenaline overflow while beating people senseless . . . which, in the course of the story, he did to Rockford, putting him in the hospital.

So, here we had a very unique mobster; one who had bipolar disease. David's idea (natch). I'm halfway through the script, and writing a scene where Rockford has been kidnapped and taken to Happy's mansion for a little interrogation and grievous bodily harm. Happy wants to know, "Why are you in my face, Rockford? Who you working for?"

I started to write the scene and I'd felt like I had written it at least half-a-dozen times before; if not on *Wiseguy*, (one of my subsequent creations), then at least on one or two of my other TV series dealing with underworld heavies.

I called David on the phone. "Help, I'm stuck," I said. "I'm working on the scene where Happy is threatening Rockford at his mansion, and it's coming out flat and ordinary."

"This is our bipolar guy, right?" David asked, clicking back into the story we'd developed a few weeks before.

"Yeah."

"Okay," David said, instantly seeing a funny twist. "What if, instead of trying to threaten Rockford, he's trying to apologize to him for the first beating, but he can't find his Lithium and instead of apologizing, everything Rockford says enrages him and he ends up almost killing him for a second time?"

"Perfect," I exclaimed.

I wrote it and it was one of the funniest scenes in the

script ... a mobster who's trying to apologize but goes berserk instead, because he can't find his Lithium. Pure David Chase.

So, that brings us to *The Sopranos*, clearly one of the most unique, groundbreaking series of this decade; a show created and produced by David Chase. This was his sole vision, his tone poem for the Millennium, as well as a salute to his New Jersey roots. He cast the actors as real people scarred by life, instead of the picture-pretty eight by ten glossies that seem to live exclusively on TV today.

He gave us, among other things, a mobster whose mother is trying to kill him for putting her in an old folks' home and a mob boss who is in analysis—no Lithium, but Prozac this time. Here, David poses the darkly funny, but very real question: What happens if your wiseguy colleagues find out you're having an emotional breakdown and are sitting in a cracked vinyl La-z-Boy twice a week, venting mob business to a head doctor?

With *The Sopranos*, we get David Chase, unfettered and in all his glory, spilling out this uncharacteristic but jewel encrusted madness, making you laugh and cry, while at the same time, wondering at his brilliant storytelling and perfect ear for dialogue.

And now, for my one comment on TV in general ...

I think it is a sad commentary on the last two decades of television that this man, who was well known to all the networks for almost twenty-five years, could not get his fresh, totally unique ideas past the guardians of our public airwaves (read network executives here). Instead of *The Sopranos*, we more often got mindless clones of last year's semi-hits, while David made his living running other people's shows, unable to sell his own.

Not until HBO finally saw his incredible gift did he get a chance to stand alone on a stage of his own making.

How could somebody who made me see my own weakness with his strengths, back in the seventies, have to wait almost thirty years to be treated to the success he so richly deserves?

Go figure.

Maybe there are those who would excuse it by saying he just needed those twenty-five years for seasoning.

But, I was there. I read that first *Rockford* script and was humbled by it. So, if you want a knowledgeable opinion from somebody who knows, I say . . .

FUGEDDABOUDIT.

—January 7, 2000

PHOTO CREDITS

vi: Photograph of James Gandolfini and Dominic Chianese at NYC premiere of *Under Hellgate Bridge* Copyright © 1999 John Barrett/ Globe Photos, Inc.

xviii: Photograph of James Gandolfini at the 2nd season premiere screening of *The Sopranos* at the State Theatre in NYC Copyright © 1996 Walter Weissman/Globe Photos, Inc.

Page 10: Photograph of Steven Van Zandt at the performance of *Hughie* Copyright © 1996 Henry McGee/Globe Photos, Inc.

Page 22: Photograph of Lorraine Bracco Copyright © 1992 Lisa Rose/Globe Photos, Inc.

Page 32: Photograph of Tony Sirico at the 2nd season premiere screening of *The Sopranos* at the Ziegfeld Theatre in NYC Copyright © 1996 Sonia Moskowitz/Globe Photos, Inc.

Page 38-39: Photograph of Michael Imperioli and Victoria at the 2nd season premiere screening of *The Sopranos* at the Ziegfeld Theatre in NYC Copyright © 1996 Sonia Moskowitz/Globe Photos, Inc.

Page 42: Photograph of *The Sopranos* creator David Chase at Manolo's restaurant in New Jersey Copyright © 1999 The New York Times/Librado Romero

Page 48-49: Photograph of David Chase and James Gandolfini at the Writers Guild in Beverly Hills, California Copyright © 1999 AP/Worldwide Photos

Page 54: Photograph of Vincent Pastore at premiere of *Mickey Blue Eyes* at the Ziegfeld Theatre in NYC Copyright © 1999 Henry McGee/Globe Photos, Inc.

Back Cover, Pages 62-63: Photograph of the cast of *The Sopranos* at the 2nd season premiere screening of *The Sopranos* at the Ziegfeld Theatre in NYC Copyright © 1996 Sonia Moskowitz/Globe Photos, Inc.

Page 68: Photograph of Edie Falco at the *51st Annual Emmy Awards* at the Shrine Auditorium in California Copyright © 1999 Alec Michael/Globe Photos, Inc.

Page 74: Photograph of Vincent Pastore and Dominic Chianese at NYC premiere of *Under Hellgate Bridge* Copyright © 1999 John Barrett/Globe Photos, Inc.

Page 82: Photograph of James Gandolfini and Steven Van Zandt at screening of *The Sopranos* at the State Theatre in NYC Copyright © 1999 Walter Weissman/Globe Photos, Inc.

Page 91: Photograph of Michael Imperioli at the National Review Board Gala Copyright © 1996 Andrea Renault/Globe Photos, Inc.

Page 92: Photograph of Edie Falco at the HBO Emmy Party at Spago, in Beverly Hills, California Copyright © 1999 Fitzroy Barrett/Globe Photos, Inc.

Page 107: Photograph of Nancy Marchand Copyright © 1981 Lynn McAffe/Globe Photos, Inc.

Page 115: Photograph of Jamie Lynn Sigler and David Proval at the 2nd season premiere screening of *The Sopranos* at the Ziegfeld Theatre in NYC Copyright © 1996 Sonia Moskowitz/Globe Photos, Inc.

Page 119: Photograph of Dominic Chianese at screening of *The Sopranos* at the State Theatre in NYC Copyright © 1999 Henry McGee/Globe Photos, Inc.